ESSENTIAL FINANCE FOR JOURNALISTS

ESSENTIAL FINANCE FOR JOURNALISTS

Edited by Brian O'Kane

OAK TREE PRESS

This book was typeset by CORK PUBLISHING
for Oak Tree Press, 4 Arran Quay, Dublin 7, Ireland.

A catalogue record is available for this book from the British Library.

ISBN 1 872853 03 X (p/b)

Printed in Ireland by
Betaprint, Ltd, Dublin

Contents

Contributors

Peter Clokey: A corporate finance partner in Price Waterhouse, responsible for finance raising and mergers and acquisitions. Previously, a director of an international merchant bank.

Mike Goolden: A chartered accountant and member of the Institute of Taxation who is the partner in charge of a Price Waterhouse corporate tax group in London. His experience covers all aspects of taxation, but his principal involvement has been with large UK and multinational groups, providing advice on tax structures and overseas tax issues.

Geoffrey Holmes: A chartered accountant and former editor of *Accountancy*, the journal of the Institute of Chartered Accountants in England and Wales, now retired after 30 years in financial journalism.

Helen Jameson: A chartered accountant with Price Waterhouse who is responsible for providing financial risk management services to financial services clients. She has specialised in banking, with particular emphasis on capital markets and risk management.

Mary Keegan: Technical partner in Price Waterhouse Audit and Business Advisory Services, responsible for accounting and reporting matters.

Brian O'Kane: A chartered accountant and former editor of *Accountancy*, the journal of the Institute of Chartered Accountants in England and Wales, now managing director of Cork Publishing Limited and editor of *Certified Accountant*, the journal of the Chartered Association of Certified Accountants.

Russ Stanfield: Qualified as a solicitor and is a tax partner in the London office of Price Waterhouse, where he heads up the estate planning and personal financial planning disciplines. He deals with all financial aspects of high net worth individuals and executives.

Additional research by Mary-Rose O'Sullivan, Cork Publishing.

Foreword

It is in everyone's interest that all journalists should have a basic understanding of financial matters. Even if you are not a financial specialist, it is more than likely that any story you are dealing with – be it the most recent decisions of the local authority, the launch of a new product, or even a human interest story – will have a financial angle.

The better-informed the journalists are, the better-served their readers will be. We were immediately enthusiastic when we heard of Brian O'Kane's plans for this book, and we have been pleased to sponsor its production and to contribute some chapters from our own expertise.

Finance is neither frightening nor boring when you have gained some understanding of it. If you become an expert, like the authors of this book, you will discover how fascinating the world of finance can be. We hope that this book will be an invaluable source of reference for you, and may even lead you to pursue the subject further.

Ian Brindle
Senior Partner
Price Waterhouse

Introduction

In early 1989, I was approached by Clifford Booth, then with the Periodicals Training Council (PTC), who was looking for a lecturer in financial matters to present a course that he was planning. I had already given notice of my intention to leave my position as editor of *Accountancy* to return with my family to Ireland and, since I was in the market for work, I volunteered my services. Since then, I have lectured on the topic several times for the PTC and its clients.

On the second or third occasion, it occurred to me that there must be some way to prevent course participants' eyes glazing over towards the end of the day with the overload of information they were receiving. I looked for a suitable 'finance for non-financial people' book to use as pre-course reading material but, from the many on the market, found nothing suited to journalists' specific needs. So I resolved to produce one myself.

David Longbottom of the PTC was quick with his encouragement and Price Waterhouse laid to rest my concerns about the book's commercial viability with their offer of the firm's sponsorship. So here it is – at last!

The aim of the book

My aim in producing this book is to provide journalists with a useful reference source on financial matters, which can be read either straight through in a single pass or dipped into to provide the answer to a specific query. The Contents page acts as a signpost for the first approach; the index for the second.

Background information on the regulation of the financial arena and those who work within it – the professions and the financial and regulatory institutions – is essential for the working financial journalist and useful for the journalist whose responsibilities extend only occasionally to financial matters.

Summary

Although this is a book on finance, the first chapter necessarily deals with legal matters. This is because the law, in its various forms, lays down the framework within which the financial world operates. For example, it would be impossible to distinguish the differing methods of presenting accounting information if one did not appreciate the distinction between a partnership and a limited company, or between a private limited company and a public company; nor would taxation make any sense without the distinction between a corporation and an individual. The chapter on *Company Law*, therefore, sets the scene for those that follow. For a broader review of the law, readers are directed to *Essential Law for Journalists*, by Tom Welsh and Walter Greenwood (ISBN 0 406 57920 2).

Financial accounting and reporting explains the legislative and regulatory framework with which financial reporting must comply, from accounting standards, through company financial reporting to auditing.

City institutions and *Regulation* are the twin pillars of the financial journalist's knowledge of how the markets operate. Brief commentary on the institutions and their role, coupled with a summary of the regulatory framework, provide an ideal source of reference.

Corporate finance, including venture capital, and *Treasury*, including the capital markets and Euromarkets, are covered in the next two chapters. Although each section could provide several books for the general reader, sufficient information can be found here to banish ignorance – which, in summary, is the aim of the book as a whole.

The chapter on *Investments* takes its cue from the Financial Services Act and concentrates on those forms of investment that are now the subject of legislation.

No book on finance would be complete without a section on taxation. This book has two: on *Business taxation* and on *Personal financial and tax planning*. Both give a summary of the legislation and the principles embodied therein, but avoid detailed references to tax rates to prevent the premature loss of value of the book from outdated information. Regular updates on tax rates and other information may be had from the sponsors, Price Waterhouse.

Finding the story in accounts is an essential chapter for every journalist. Because it is written from a journalist's point of view, by an author who has written as a financial journalist for over 30 years, it offers an insight not to be found elsewhere.

Finally, again with the journalist in mind, this book ends with a *Glossary*, an explanation of acronyms used in the text and a directory of sources, complete with telephone numbers.

Thank yous and caveats

My sincere thanks go to David Longbottom of the PTC and Sue Hurley of Price Waterhouse for their early and continued encouragement; Valerie Moores, who throughout the project, provided an unfailing entrée to the resources of Price Waterhouse; the authors for sharing their expert knowledge in such a readable form; and my wife and family, to whom this book is dedicated, for their love.

Any book that summarises as broad and as deep a topic as this book does runs the risk of simplifying to the point of error. The authors have worked within their brief; any errors and omissions should be laid at my door alone.

And last, a warning that the contents of this book are subject to change after publication. New editions will be published, as appropriate, to keep the material as up to date as possible.

Brian O'Kane
Cork
October 1993

Company law

A journalist with an interest in finance needs to know something about the legal framework within which the financial world operates. For example, it would be impossible to distinguish the differing methods of presenting accounting information if one did not appreciate the distinction between a partnership and a limited company, or between a private limited company and a public company; nor would taxation make any sense without the distinction between a company and an individual. This chapter, therefore, looks at those aspects of company law that help towards an understanding of finance.

Choice of business structure

The forms of business entity, through which entrepreneurs may choose to conduct their enterprise, are:

- Sole trader
- Partnership
- Limited company
- Unlimited company
- Company limited by guarantee
- Co-operative.

Sole traders

Sole traders are not subject to any restriction on their establishment or manner of operation. A sole trader can start in business without any formality, can run several different businesses without distinguishing between the income and expenses of each, and need not make available to the public any financial information about his business activities.

However, a sole trader carries unlimited liability, which means that the owner of the business is personally liable for all the debts of the business, if it fails, since the business debts cannot be distinguished from personal debts. Because of the risk to which this exposes the sole trader, it is unusual to find any sizeable enterprise being carried on in this way.

Partnerships

A partnership exists where two or more individuals have expressly, or implicitly by their actions, agreed to act together for a common purpose. Except in Scotland, where the law is different, the partnership is indivisible from the individuals involved and ceases when one partner leaves or another joins.

Partners are jointly and severally liable for the debts of the firm. This means that not only is each partner jointly liable for the debts of the firm but that any individual partner may be liable for any debts of the firm that cannot be satisfied from the partnership assets.

Under the Limited Partnership Act 1907, one or more partners may invest in a firm with limited liability, provided there is at least one partner with unlimited liability (the general partner). Since the general partner is somewhat exposed in this situation, it is unsurprising that limited partnerships are not popular for trading enterprises. Limited partnerships are sometimes used for tax planning purposes, where the partnership aspect gives rise to tax advantages not available by other means and limited liability need not be foregone.

Partnerships are regulated by the Partnership Act 1890 and by any partnership agreement entered into by the partners concerned. Typically, a partnership agreement extends the regulation provided by statute and deals with matters such as profit-sharing and capital contributions between partners.

Partnerships (except of accountants and lawyers) may not consist of more than 20 people. Companies may be partners. Where the name of the partnership does not consist of the names of all the partners concerned, the names of the partners must appear on all business stationery (or a note indicating where a full list of partners' names may be inspected). The effective business address of the partnership (equivalent to a company's registered office) must also appear on stationery.

Like sole traders, partnerships are not required to make public any financial information.

Limited companies

The principal difference between a limited company and the other forms of business entity lies in the extent of the liability of the owners.

If an individual incurs a debt, he is liable to repay it to the full extent of his resources; likewise, a business that incurs debts must repay them to the full extent of its resources. Limited liability, a concept developed in the 19th century, sets a limit on the liability of the owners of a business for the debts of the business and distinguishes between those assets that they have committed to the business and those which remain separate from it.

The liability of one of the owners of a company limited by shares is restricted to the amount invested in the share capital of the company or, if this has not been fully paid up, to the amount agreed to be invested. In this way, the owners are protected from losing everything they own in the event of the failure of a company in which they have a shareholding.

However, more than just the shareholders need to be protected if business is to be encouraged. Those who deal with the company, particularly those who extend credit to the company – its bankers or trade creditors, for example – need to be reassured that the owners of the business will not use the limited liability they enjoy to the detriment of third parties.

This is achieved in two ways:

- Increasingly strict legislation as to the responsibilities and duties of directors of limited companies and heavy penalties for non-compliance with, or breaches of, the legislation
- A requirement for regular formal disclosure of information relating to the financial performance and condition of the company.

Unlimited companies

Limited liability companies are the most common form of business entity. Unlimited companies – that is, companies whose owners choose not to limit their liability to meet the debts of the company in the event of its failure – are typically used for charitable or not-for-profit enterprises, where limited liability status would not be appropriate but the disciplines of company-style financial reporting are desired. Such a company will, in its Memorandum of Association (see below), have a clause stating "The liability of the members is unlimited".

Companies limited by guarantee

In the case of a charity or not-for-profit enterprise, those involved may want the disciplines imposed by company-style reporting but may feel that unlimited liability is too risky personally while limited liability might give a wrong impression to third parties. In this instance, they may opt for a company limited by guarantee.

Here, the liability of the members is limited to the amount they agree, on becoming members, to pay up in the event of the failure of the company. Typically, this amount is minimal – perhaps only £1, or even 5p – and thus the effect of limited liability is achieved, reducing personal risk, while the words "by guarantee" suggest that third parties are not themselves at risk. The subterfuge is innocent (usually) and this form of business entity is rarely used for trading businesses.

Foreign companies

A foreign company may incorporate a UK subsidiary company (limited or unlimited, private or public) through which to do business in the United Kingdom. However, it is also able to register its presence here as a 'branch' or 'place of business'.

Branch

A foreign company should register a branch in Great Britain where it performs any functions here which are anything other than ancillary or incidental to the company's main business, and the branch is able to conduct business in this country on behalf of the foreign company. Having registered a branch, a person resident in Great Britain will be able to deal directly with the branch as if he were dealing with the company in its home State.

To register a branch it is necessary, within one month of establishing the branch, to file with the Registrar of Companies a Form BR1, together with a certified copy of the statutes of the company, translated if they are not in English. It is also necessary to file a copy of the company's latest annual accounts together with a £50 registration fee.

The branch must arrange for copies of the company's accounts, not just the branch accounts, to be filed with the Registrar of Companies on an annual basis. The format of these accounts will depend upon the requirements in its country of incorporation concerning format, disclosure and auditing. They must be filed within three months after the date on which they are made public in its country of incorporation, unless the foreign company is not required to prepare, audit and disclose its accounts in its home state. In these cases, the Registrar of Companies will accept a simple balance sheet and profit and loss account (with comparatives for the previous year), which must be filed within 13 months of the accounting reference date, together with a £32 filing fee.

Place of business

Where the foreign company's activities in the UK are only ancillary or incidental to its overseas business, it can register a place of business instead of registering a branch. Ancillary and incidental activities would include a share registration office or administrative functions such as warehousing.

A place of business must be registered within one month of setting up here by filing a Form 691 (which includes a statutory declaration stating the date on which the place of business was established), and a certified copy of the statutes of the foreign company, translated if they are not in English. There is a registration fee of £50. A Form 701A should be filed to notify the accounting reference date of the foreign company.

Foreign companies with a place of business in the UK must file accounts with the Registrar of Companies. These accounts will be the accounts of the company as a whole, not just the place of business, and may be in the form prescribed under its home company law. If none are required by the foreign law, company accounts must be prepared consisting, as a minimum, of a balance sheet and profit and loss account together with comparatives for the previous year. They need not be audited. The accounts must be filed with the Registrar of Companies within 13 months of the company's accounting reference date, and a filing fee of £32 is payable.

Both the branch and the place of business registration regimes require the foreign company to disclose other information about itself, such as charges given over its property, changes in accounting reference date and changes in officers (directors, company secretaries and representatives, etc). There are additional disclosure and registration requirements for credit and financial institutions.

Company formation

Probably the single most important reason for forming a limited company is to avail of the protection of limited liability. By forming a limited company as the vehicle through which a business will be managed, the shareholders can protect those other assets they own that they have not invested in the company.

The second most important reason is taxation. The tax treatment of profits earned by limited companies can, in some circumstances, be more favourable than the treatment of similar profits in other forms of business entity.

Other reasons for forming a limited company are:

- Acceptability: A limited company is the most usual form of business entity and is considered an acceptable vehicle through which to manage a business
- Prestige: The formation of a limited company by an entrepreneur indicates a commitment to his/her enterprise which is accorded a high degree of prestige by the market
- Protection of name: If the name under which you wish to trade gives a competitive advantage, one way to protect it is to form a company with that name (though the best way is to register the name as a trade mark).

There are disadvantages, too. The principal disadvantages are:

- The need to prepare, and have audited, annual accounts in a prescribed format

- The need to disclose information about the business by filing accounts and an Annual Return with the Registrar of Companies for public inspection
- In certain circumstances, the tax treatment of income earned through a company and passed to shareholders or directors as fees or salaries may be less favourable than if the income was earned by the individual direct.

Forming a limited company

The steps involved are:

- Decide on a name for the company
- Define the purpose for which the company is being formed
- Prepare the Memorandum of Association
- Prepare the Articles of Association
- Submit the appropriate forms (No 10, No 12), together with the Memorandum and Articles of Association and a cheque or draft for the registration fee (currently £50) to the Registrar of Companies.

If the application to form a company is accepted, the Registrar of Companies will issue a Certificate of Incorporation. Only after its issue may the company begin to trade, though a public company also needs a Certificate of Trading.

Broadly, the same steps are followed to form an unlimited company or a company limited by guarantee.

Company names

In choosing a name, care must be taken to avoid one that:

- Is identical to the name of an existing company
- Could be confused with the name of an existing company, because it is phonetically identical or the difference in spelling is such as to be immaterial
- Infringes on an existing trade mark
- In the opinion of the Secretary of State for Trade and Industry is offensive or would constitute a criminal offence
- Contains the words, 'Limited', 'Unlimited', 'Public Limited Company' (or abbreviations thereof or their Welsh equivalents) other than at the end of the name.

Approval of the Secretary of State for Trade and Industry is required (usually obtained through the relevant section in the Department of Trade and Industry) for names that include words that imply:

- National or international pre-eminence (for example, British, International)
- Governmental patronage or sponsorship (for example, Authority, Council)
- Business pre-eminence or representative status (for example, Association, Institute)
- Specific objects or functions (for example, Building Society, Stock Exchange)
- A connection with the government or a local authority.

Permission is also required for names that are included on a list of words requiring special approval. Among these are:

- Royal
- Police
- Nursing
- Charity
- University
- Credit Union
- Bank.

The company's name must be displayed outside every office or place of business, in a conspicuous position. It must also appear on all business letters, invoices, notices, etc.

Company objects

The formal description of a company's purpose (the reason why it was formed) is contained in the company's 'objects'.

The objects are to be found in the company's Memorandum of Association (part of its constitution). The clause summarises the purposes for which the company was formed; only these purposes may be pursued by the directors and management of the company. Extending the business beyond the objects set for it, without first amending them, risks making the directors personally liable for the debts of the company. In this situation, the company is said to be acting *ultra vires* – that is, outside its powers.

In addition, an *ultra vires* contract entered into by the company cannot be enforced by the company against the other party to the contract, though that other party can enforce it against the company.

To reduce the risk of transactions being held to be *ultra vires*, most companies' objects clauses are widely drawn. Even when tied to a specific industry, sufficient latitude is usually left to prevent any danger of exceeding the boundaries of action.

Scope is provided by clauses like these:

'To undertake, provide and carry out any service or contract of works deemed necessary or advantageous in promoting the objects of the company',

or:

'To do all such things as are incidental or conducive to the above objects or any of them'.

Memorandum and Articles of Association

The Memorandum of Association, together with the Articles of Association, forms the constitution of a company.

The Memorandum consists of:

- A clause giving the name of the company, with 'Limited' as the last word of the name
- The objects clause
- A statement that the company is a private company (or a public limited company, if that is the case)
- A clause stating that the liability of the members of the company is limited
- A clause setting out the amount and subdivision of the company's share capital
- A statement that the company's registered office is located in England and Wales or in Scotland
- The names and addresses of the subscribers – the first shareholders – and the number of shares each has agreed to take (each must take at least one share).

The Memorandum is usually signed by at least two subscribers, although new regulations, permitting the formation of private limited companies with only one shareholder, came into force in 1992. Subscribers' names and addresses must be stated and their signatures witnessed and dated. Each subscriber must write opposite his name the number of shares he has agreed to take.

Where the Memorandum of Association of a company sets the broad sweep of the company's purpose, the Articles of Association spell out the internal regulations of the company.

The main contents of the Articles of Association are:

- A reference to 'Table A' (see below)
- Share capital: Procedures for its allotment and issue, the issue of different classes of share capital with or without different rights
- General meetings of the company: The manner of proposing resolutions and the periods of notice attaching thereto, the manner of voting, where the meetings shall take place

- Borrowing powers: Whether any limits apply, other than those to be later imposed by the company's bankers
- Directors: The manner and period of their appointment, the basis of their remuneration, their number, and how often Board meetings are held
- Any indemnities given by the company to directors or officers of the company
- Dividend provisions
- Winding up provisions.

The subscribers to the Memorandum of Association – the first shareholders – also sign their names to the Articles of Association.

The Companies Regulations 1985 includes a standard format Articles of Association (Part I, Table A, First Schedule). This is known as Table A, and is deemed to apply unless it is excluded by the Articles. It is adopted in full by most companies, in preference to drafting their own Articles.

Share capital

Every limited company (except those limited by guarantee) has share capital. This is the money that the shareholders have invested in the business. It may not be repaid, except in certain specific instances, until the company is wound up.

Authorised share capital is the maximum amount that the shareholders can invest; the amount that they actually invest is called the Issued share capital.

There is no minimum authorised share capital for a private limited company. A public limited company must have a minimum issued share capital of £50,000, of which at least a quarter of the nominal value of the shares together with any premium must be paid up.

Each shareholder must receive a certificate for his shareholding. It is not necessary to issue an individual certificate for each share. However, unless the directors or shareholders resolve to dispense with numbering, it must be possible from the certificate to identify the shares held.

Types of share capital

Most companies, particularly small private companies, have a single class of ordinary share capital with a single vote for each share held. Classes of shares, other than 'Ordinary' shares, include:

- Preference shares
- Redeemable shares
- Cumulative preference shares
- Participating preference shares
- Convertible shares.

Preference shares
Preference shares have priority over 'Ordinary' shares in the payment of dividends and/or the return of capital in the event that the company is dissolved. In addition, preference shares usually earn a fixed return. Thus, a '7 per cent' preference share will earn a dividend equivalent to a 7 per cent return on the nominal value of the share capital and this will be paid before dividends on ordinary shares are paid. Because of this, preference shares are often regarded as loan rather than equity capital.

Redeemable shares
Redeemable preference shares, unlike ordinary shares, may be redeemed by the company – that is, bought back from their owners. The agreement under which these shares are issued will explain whether redemption is at the company's and/or the holder's option, whether it is to take place on a fixed date or during a period, and whether a premium (or bonus) is payable on redemption.

Cumulative preference shares
Although preference shares generally have their dividend paid before ordinary shares, this may be of little comfort to the preference shareholder who is told that no dividend is being paid this year. Cumulative preference shares 'roll up' any unpaid dividends and these rank for payment before preference dividends for the current year. Thus, arrears of preference dividends have to be met before ordinary shareholders can be paid any dividend and should be disclosed in the company's accounts.

Participating preference shares
Preference shareholders may also feel unhappy with a fixed dividend, especially in years where profits are good and ordinary shareholders are paid high dividends. Participating preference shares are paid additional dividends, after ordinary shareholders have received a certain amount. For example, a participating preference share might be paid a 7 per cent dividend plus one half of the ordinary dividend where the total amount payable in dividends exceeds £500,000.

Convertible preference shares
Convertible preference shares are convertible into ordinary shares on a basis agreed at the time of their issue. The agreement will specify whether conversion is at the company's and/or the holder's option, the price at which conversion is to take place, whether conversion is to take place on a fixed date or during a period and whether conversion is to take place only on the occurrence of specific circumstances. For example, shares may be convertible after five years at the company's option at a price of 57p; alternatively, shares may be convertible if the

company fails to achieve certain predetermined profit targets. Usually, investors seek convertible preference shares in order to be able to share in a company's growth, while having a guaranteed return in the early years.

Subject to the company's Articles of Association, which may vary the voting rights between different classes of share, each shareholder has a vote, in proportion to his shareholding, in the running of the company. This vote may be exercised at the Annual General Meeting, or at any Extraordinary General Meetings that may be called. Because of the shareholder's right to receive information from the company and attend meetings, many City editors and financial journalists hold small shareholdings (perhaps, even a single share) in the companies that they feel are worth watching. Beware here for two pitfalls:

- The cost of buying a single share may be disproportionate to the value of the share itself
- If your job involves 'tipping' (that is, recommending shares for investors to buy or sell), holding shares in companies which you might tip is a definite 'No! No!'. This is because it would be easy for an influential journalist to manipulate the share price of a company in which he held shares, to his own advantage.

The shareholders

The shareholders are the owners of the company. Each is entitled to a proportion, related to their shareholding, of the dividends declared by the directors of the company each year, as well as a similar proportion of the assets, including profits not paid out as dividends, of the company when and if it is wound up.

In small companies, the shareholders are often the directors and manage the business themselves. However, in law, a distinction is drawn between the owners of a business – the shareholders – and the managers – the directors. The latter must account to the former for their actions.

An individual's shareholding in a company is evidenced by a share certificate. This is a valuable document since it is evidence of ownership of the shares. Shares may not be transferred or sold without surrender of the share certificate, together with the appropriate signed and stamped stock transfer form.

Unless a shareholder is employed by the company, as a director or executive, he has no right to interfere in the day-to-day management of the business.

Usually, companies must have at least two shareholders though new legislation permits the formation of private limited companies with only one shareholder. This recognises the situation of many small companies where a husband and wife are the shareholders – one being active in the business and the other merely a figure-head to satisfy legal requirements.

The directors

The directors of a company are appointed by the shareholders to run the business. In most small companies, the shareholders and directors are the same people. In larger companies, many of the directors will have only a few shares or even no shareholding at all; they are effectively employed managers.

The directors are officers of the company and responsible to the shareholders for the efficient management of the company. They must:

- Carry out their duties at all times with the best interests of the company in mind
- Not make secret profits from their position as directors
- Account regularly to the shareholders for their actions.

The activities of company directors are under increasing regulation. For example, insolvency legislation provides for a review of directors' actions in the period prior to the collapse of the company; if the directors, or any one of them, can be shown to have acted improperly, an application can be made to the courts to have that person or persons disqualified from holding a position as director in future.

In addition, the role of directors, particularly of quoted companies, has been a subject of much debate in the past year or so. The Cadbury Committee (The Committee on the Financial Aspects of Corporate Governance, set up in May 1991 by the Financial Reporting Council, The Stock Exchange and the accountancy profession) has recommended a formal code of conduct for both executive and non-executive company directors. Under the proposals in the 'Cadbury report', quoted companies would explain each year in their annual accounts to what extent their directors had complied with the code. The proposals are still being debated, with commentators divided on whether they are too onerous or not far-reaching enough. (See also the section on Corporate governance in the chapter on *Regulation*.)

Most directors are executive directors. This means that they have a full time responsibility to the company as, for example, finance director or managing director. Some companies appoint directors who have no day-to-day involvement with the company – these are non-executive directors. Non-executive directors are held to be valuable because of their independence. Much of the debate referred to above centres on the use of non-executive directors and the reality of their independence. It is often instructive to look at a company's board of directors as shown in the Annual Report and identify the number and quality of the non-executive directors.

The first directors of a company are appointed by the subscribers to the Memorandum and Articles of Association. Although the formal powers to appoint directors remains with the shareholders, it is common practice for new directors to be co-opted by the Board. A corporate body may be appointed as a director.

Form No 10 – one of the forms used to apply for the incorporation of a company – is used to record the appointment of the first directors and the first Secretary, as well as the intended location of the company's registered office.

Note that the consent of the directors, as evidenced by their signatures on Form No 10, is required before their appointment is valid. Directors must also disclose their residential address, date of birth, nationality, business occupation and details of any other directorships held by them in the UK in the last five years.

Changes in directors, or in their particulars, are notified to the Registrar of Companies on Form No. 288, within 14 days of the change.

Directors may have shareholdings in their companies, if the holdings are disclosed to the Board. Market wisdom has it that when directors increase their holdings, the company is a good bet, and when directors sell, it is time for others to do so, too. However, directors must be aware of the restrictions of the Companies Securities (Insider Dealing) Act, 1985 (see chapter on *Regulation*); in addition, directors of quoted companies are forbidden by The Stock Exchange from buying or selling shares in their company except at certain times. This is to prevent directors taking advantage of their knowledge of future events and transactions to make profits at the expense of other shareholders. On Saturdays, the *Financial Times* publishes a listing of directors' transactions in major quoted companies, compiled by the Directus consultancy.

The Secretary

The Secretary, like the directors, is an officer of the company. The Secretary and the directors are responsible for ensuring the legal 'persona' of the company is kept alive. He is responsible for filing with the Registrar of Companies the various forms and documents needed during a company's life.

The Secretary is often also a director of the company, although where a transaction requires the signatures of a director and the Secretary, the same person cannot sign under both positions. A company may have more than one Secretary and a corporate body may be appointed as Secretary.

The first Secretary is appointed by the subscribers to the Memorandum and Articles of Association. Form No 10 is used to record his appointment. Note that the consent of the Secretary, as evidenced by the signature on Form No 10, is required before his appointment is valid. Changes in Secretary are notified to the Registrar of Companies on Form No. 288, within 14 days of the change.

Private limited companies

A private limited company, since July 1992, need only have a single shareholder (previously, two); in addition, previous restrictions on the maximum numbers of shareholders no longer apply.

Public limited companies

Public limited companies may carry the abbreviation 'plc' (or P.L.C., or some other variant, including the Welsh equivalent) at the end of their names. At least two members are required and a minimum share capital of £50,000, a quarter of the nominal value of which must be paid up, together with the whole of any premium.

A plc is subject to tighter regulation than a private limited company. This is because a plc has the right to offer its shares or debentures to members of the public. To do so, a 'prospectus', a formal offer document whose content is tightly controlled, is required.

Note that while companies cannot be listed on The Stock Exchange unless they are plcs, plc status of itself does not mean that a company is listed or 'quoted'. The phrase 'public company' is often used (wrongly) where 'quoted company' is meant; and a company may be described as 'private', when what is meant is 'not publicly quoted'. Beware of these nuances.

Re-registration

It is possible for a private company to re-register at Companies House as a public company and vice versa.

To re-register a private company as a public company, it is necessary to hold a shareholders' meeting to pass special resolutions to alter the company's Memorandum and Articles of Association. The company must also satisfy the relevant capital requirement of a public company. Within 15 days of the resolutions being passed, the company must file with the Registrar of Companies:

- An application to re-register as a public company
- Copies of the special resolutions
- A printed copy of the altered Memorandum and Articles of Association
- A copy of a balance sheet (and unqualified audit report) for a date not more than seven months prior to the application

- A written statement from the auditors in relation to the net assets position in the balance sheet
- The re-registration fee, currently £50.

In some circumstances, other valuation reports are also required.

If the Registrar of Companies is satisfied that the company meets the statutory requirements, he will issue a Certificate of Incorporation on re-registration as a public company, and the company will become a public company from the date on this certificate.

The procedures for re-registering a public company as a private company are less onerous as the regulation of private companies is less demanding. The public company must hold a shareholders' meeting to approve the special resolutions to re-register as a private company, and alter the company's Memorandum and Articles of Association. The company must file with the Registrar of Companies, within 15 days, copies of the special resolutions together with an application to re-register as a private company, a printed copy of the altered Memorandum and Articles of Association and a filing fee, currently £50.

A new Certificate of Incorporation on re-registration will be issued 28 days from the passing of the resolution, and the company will become a private company from that date.

Private limited companies can re-register as unlimited and vice versa, however, these types of re-registration are rare and a company cannot reverse such re-registrations. All the shareholders of a limited company must give their consent before it may re-register as unlimited.

The Company Seal

It is no longer necessary for every company to have a seal but, where one exists, it must be used and the name of the company engraved on it in legible characters. A seal embosses the characters of the company's name onto any document stamped by it.

The use of the company seal is usually restricted to important documents, such as share certificates, trust deeds, contracts, mortgages and the like. When not in use, the seal is kept in safe custody. It should only be used with the authority of the directors. Sealed documents should be countersigned by two directors, or a director and the Secretary. There must be only one seal unless the Articles allow for a further seal to be used – for example, by the company's Registrars for sealing share certificates.

Certificate of Incorporation

A company does not formally exist until a Certificate of Incorporation has been issued by the Registrar of Companies.

This certificate is a valuable document and must not be defaced or altered in any way.

Registered number

For official purposes, a company is distinguished not just by its name but also by a number. This is its Registered Number which will never change, unlike the name of the company which may be altered at any time by the shareholders. It appears on the Certificate of Incorporation and is assigned by the Registrar of Companies.

A company's Registered Number must be shown on all invoices and other correspondence.

The company's Registered Number has no connection with the numbers issued by the Inland Revenue for VAT, PAYE/National Insurance or Corporation Tax.

Publication in the *London Gazette*

The Registrar of Companies will publish an announcement of the formation of a new company in the *London Gazette*, the official bulletin of companies' activities, which is available from HMSO weekly, price £1.40.

This announcement allows members of the public to check the company's record at the Companies Office to see who the shareholders and directors of the company are, what the company's objects are, and all the other information recorded on file.

The first meeting

The first meeting of the Board of Directors of a newly formed limited company is of importance because, at that meeting, certain decisions are taken which are binding on the company.

The meeting usually follows a standard format:

- The Certificate of Incorporation of the company is produced to the directors
- The Memorandum and Articles of Association are produced to the directors
- The company seal, if any, is adopted
- The directors are confirmed in their appointment
- The Secretary is confirmed in his/her appointment
- Shares are issued to the shareholders
- The auditors are appointed
- A resolution is passed, in the form specified by the bank, authorising a bank chosen by the directors to open and maintain an account on behalf of the company

- An 'accounting reference date' is chosen, which is the date to which the first accounts will be prepared.

If the company has been bought 'off the shelf' (that is, already formed), further items of business are necessary at the meeting:
- The first directors and Secretary – usually the company registration agent and members of his staff – resign and new directors and a new Secretary are appointed
- The shareholdings of the subscribers to the Memorandum and Articles of Association – again, usually the company registration agent and members of his staff – are transferred to the new owners of the company.

At the first meeting, additional directors may be appointed.

Company administration

Once the company has been formed and is trading, there is a continuing obligation on the company to file information on its activities. This administration work is the duty of the Secretary.

The statutory books

A company's statutory books are those registers it is required by legislation to keep. They include:
- The Register of Members (also known as the Share Register)
- The Register of Directors
- The Register of Secretaries
- The Register of Directors' Interests and copies of directors' service contracts of more than twelve months
- The Register of Charges
- The Register of Debenture Holders
- The Minute Book.

The Register of Members

The Register of Members is a key document, which provides a formal record of all the shareholders in a company.

A person does not legally become a shareholder in a company until his name has been entered in the Register of Members, nor does he cease to be a shareholder until an entry is made in the register transferring his shares to a third party. The Secretary is therefore obliged to ensure that the Register of Members is kept up to date at all times.

The Register of Members must be kept at the company's registered office, unless notice of a change in location has been filed with the Registrar of Companies.

The Register must be available for inspection by any shareholder of the company for at least two hours daily during business hours, and likewise by any other person on payment of a fee not exceeding £2.50 per hour or part thereof.

If a shareholder, or any other person, requests a copy of the Register or any part of it, the Secretary must send it to him within 10 days. A fee of £2.50 for the first 1,000 entries, £20 for the next 1,000 entries and £15 for every subsequent 1,000 entries.

The details of the subscribers to the Memorandum and Articles of Association of the company should be the first entries in the Register of Members.

The Register of Directors

The Register of Directors must be kept at the company's registered office. It must be open to inspection by any shareholder without charge for at least two hours daily during business hours, and likewise by any other person, on payment of a fee of £2.50 per hour or part thereof.

The names and details of all directors must be included in the register. Changes in directors, or in their particulars, must be notified to the Registrar of Companies within 14 days of the change. Form No 288 is used for this purpose.

The changes that must be notified are:

- Names, whether on marriage or by deed poll
- Address
- Date of birth
- Business occupation
- Nationality
- Other directorships held in the UK in the last five years.

The Register of Secretaries

The Register of Secretaries must be kept at the company's registered office. It must be open to inspection by any shareholder without charge for at least two hours daily during business hours, and likewise by any other person, on payment of a fee of £2.50 per hour or part thereof.

Changes in the Secretary, or in his particulars, must be notified to the Registrar of Companies within 14 days of the change. Form No 288 is used for this purpose.

The changes that must be notified are:

- Names, whether on marriage or by deed poll
- Address.

The Register of Directors' Interests

The Register of Directors' Interests records the shareholdings of directors in the company. Directors' loans to the company secured by debentures are also recorded here.

The directors must notify the company on their appointment of any shareholding they have in the company and must notify any changes in this holding within five days of the change. It is this record that provides the source of the list of directors' interests which forms part of a company's Annual Report.

Directors' interests include shareholdings in the name of spouses and children under 18.

The Register of Charges

A charge is a right of security over an asset. This means that, if the company's fleet of vehicles is charged to secure the loan used to buy them, the vehicles may be taken by the lender and sold to recover the amounts owing, should the company default on its repayments.

It is clear, therefore, that a charge on assets is not to be given lightly. In order to ensure that it is not given without the knowledge of the shareholders and third parties who may provide finance to the company (whether as lender or creditor), a company is required to keep a Register of Charges, whether or not any of its assets are charged.

The Register of Charges, and copies of all instruments (that is, legal documents) creating charges on any of the company's assets, must be kept at the company's registered office and be made available for inspection by any shareholder or creditor without charge for at least two hours daily during business hours, and likewise by any other person, on payment of a fee not exceeding 5p.

In order to protect creditors and those who deal with the company, details of a charge and the original instrument creating it must be filed by the company with the Registrar of Companies within 21 days of its creation, on Form No 395, 397 (debentures), or 400 (mortgages on property). No extension beyond the 21 day period can be given by the Registrar and only an application to the High Court can provide an extension where the registration cannot be made within the time limit prescribed. In practice, chargeholders arrange the registration of charges.

When the charge is lifted, a 'memorandum of satisfaction' is filed on Form No 403a or 403b.

The Minute Book

The Minute Book is used to record the decisions arrived at by the directors at Board meetings; there is usually a separate book to record the proceedings of general meetings. Although a company's Minute Book is not open to public inspection, the book contains minutes of general meetings is open to inspection by shareholders.

Meetings

There are two main types of company meetings: directors' (or Board) meetings and General (or shareholders') meetings.

Directors' meetings

In addition to the day-to-day management of the company, directors' meetings deal with other matters such as the co-option of further directors and the appointment of bankers. Decision on matters such as employee remuneration are often delegated to a committee of the Board which would then report their decisions to the next full Board meeting.

The chairman of the board is normally one of the directors and his appointment is usually decided by the Board as a whole. Notice of Board meetings must be given to all directors unless they are abroad. The conduct of board meetings is regulated by the Articles of Association of the company which will also specify the directors' voting rights. However, the general rule is that every director has at least one vote and the chairman often has the casting vote in the event of a stalemate. Typically, the minimum number of attendees (otherwise known as the quorum) to make a directors' meeting valid is two.

General meetings

Every company is required to hold an Annual General Meeting (AGM), which must be held every calendar year, although no more than 15 months must elapse between AGMs. Private limited companies are permitted to dispense with the need to hold AGMs by passing an elective resolution. AGMs specifically deal with the company's statutory accounts, the re-appointment of auditors for the forthcoming year and the declaration of any final dividends.

General meetings other than AGMs are known as Extraordinary General Meetings (EGMs). If the quorum is not obtained within half an hour of the start time of the meeting, no business may be transacted at that meeting and it must be adjourned to a future date.

Notice of meetings

Depending on the business to be considered at general meetings, different periods of notice are required to be given to the shareholders. For example, an AGM requires at least 21 clear days notice, whereas an EGM to consider an ordinary resolution will only require 14 clear days notice. This notice may be waived by the members so long as a specified percentage of those entitled to vote actually give their consent.

AGMs require 100 per cent consent and all other general meetings require a majority in number of shareholders having a right to attend and vote together holding 95 per cent in nominal value of the shares. Every shareholder who has paid all monies due on his shares is entitled to receive notice and attend general meetings.

Unless the Articles of Association of the company provide otherwise, every shareholder has one vote which he may cast either in person at the meeting or by proxy. Voting on resolution is initially carried out by a show of hands of those present at the meeting (excluding those acting as proxies). If the outcome of the vote is clear-cut, the chairman will declare a result. However, if the chairman is in doubt as to whether there is a clear majority on a show of hands, he may call a poll. Alternatively, a prescribed number of shareholders may demand a poll. In the event of a poll, all votes cast by proxy are also taken into account and a final result is either declared at the meeting or at a specified later date.

Resolutions

A company's decisions, whether made by directors or shareholders, are made by passing resolutions. At general meetings, the type of resolution to be passed depends on the nature of the business concerned. Generally, it will be one of three types:

- Ordinary
- Special
- Extraordinary.

Unless a resolution is special or extraordinary, it is deemed to be ordinary and may be passed by a simple majority of more than 50% of votes cast.

Certain matters, including a change in the company's Articles of Association or a change of name, must be decided by way of a special resolution which may only be passed if at least 75 per cent of the votes cast are in favour.

Matters to be dealt with by way of an extraordinary resolution include the decision for a company to be wound-up. An extraordinary resolution may only be passed if at least 75 per cent of the votes cast are in favour of the resolution.

A further distinction among these three types of resolutions concerns the period of notice required to be given to the shareholders. Ordinary or extraordinary resolutions require 14 clear days notice, whereas a special resolution requires at least 21 clear days notice.

All special and extraordinary resolutions and some ordinary resolutions must be filed with the Registrar of Companies within 15 days of the date on which they are passed. In addition, every company must keep minutes of all meetings in order to enable various parties to exercise their rights of inspection.

It is possible for the directors and the shareholders of a company to reach their decisions without meeting in person. This is achieved by passing written resolutions. Written resolutions may only be passed with unanimous consent, unlike resolutions considered at meetings where only the votes cast by those present at the meeting are taken into account. Where the shareholders of a company pass written resolutions, the company is required to notify its auditors who will then consider whether the business in question should be considered in general meeting for full discussion. If after seven days of receipt of the notice, the auditors have not advised the company that a general meeting should be held, the written resolution will be valid. Such resolutions must be entered in the company's general minute book.

Shareholders of private limited companies may pass an elective resolution to dispense with certain formalities, such as:

- The need to hold future AGMs
- The need to lay accounts before the company in general meeting
- The obligation to appoint auditors annually.

This procedure is not available to public companies and may only be passed with the unanimous consent of all the company's shareholders. An elective resolution may be passed either in general meeting or by way of a written resolution. In either case, a copy of the elective resolution must be filed with the Registrar of Companies within 15 days of the date on which it has been passed.

An elective resolution may be revoked at any time by the shareholders of the company by passing an ordinary resolution and it is automatically revoked if a company re-registers as a public company.

Registered office

A company's registered office is its official 'home'. Any document delivered there is deemed in law to have been successfully delivered to the company. Therefore, those dealing with the company need:

- To know where the company's registered office is
- To be kept informed of any changes in location.

A change in the registered office of a company is only effective from the filing of Form No. 287, notifying the change. This must be filed with the Registrar of Companies within 14 days of the change.

The company's Registered Office must always be shown on its letterheads, invoices and other business stationery.

Accounts

A company must file statutory accounts every year, prepared to its notified year-end. In most cases, these must be audited and will comprise a directors' report, audit report, profit and loss account, balance sheet and notes to the accounts. These accounts must be filed at Companies House within seven months of the year-end for a public company and within ten months of the year-end for a private company. (If the company in question does business or has interests overseas, it is able to apply for a three month extension of the filing period.)

Since 1 July 1992, there are penalties on companies that do not file their accounts on time. The scale of these charges varies with the length of delay in filing and the type of company, as follows:

	Number of months delayed			
	Up to 3	**3 to 6**	**6 to 12**	**over 12**
Public companies	£500	£1,000	£2,000	£5,000
Private companies	£100	£250	£500	£1,000

Accounts are normally prepared for a period of 12 months to the accounting reference date. It is possible to shorten the period (no minimum) or extend it (maximum, 18 months). The company's first accounts may be for any period between six and 18 months; the filing deadline for a period less than or equal to 12 months is as stated above. If the first accounting period exceeds 12 months, the deadline for the filing of the accounts will be 22 months from the day of incorporation.

It is possible for small or medium-sized companies to file modified accounts at Companies House. These modified (or abbreviated) accounts will consist of the following:

- Small company accounts: Abbreviated balance sheet and a special auditors' report
- Medium company accounts: Full balance sheet, an abbreviated profit and loss account (disclosure of turnover is not required), a special auditors' report and a directors' report.

In order to qualify as a small or medium-sized company, a company must meet two or more of the following conditions:

	Small	**Medium**
Turnover	<£2.8 million	< £11.2 million
Balance Sheet total	< £1.4 million	< £5.6 million
Number of employees	< 50	< 250

Unlimited companies do not have to file accounts at Companies House unless they are a subsidiary or holding company of a limited company.

Dormant companies, that is those having no accounting transactions whatsoever during the year, are able to pass a special resolution (under Section 250 of the *Companies Act* 1985) to dispense with the requirement to appoint auditors. The filing deadline for these unaudited accounts, and late filing penalties, apply as for audited accounts.

The Annual Return

A company must file an Annual Return. This updates and confirms its record at Companies House for changes in directors, shareholders, etc.

When a 'company search' (that is, a check of the information held in Companies House on a company) is done, the most up-to-date information can be obtained from the latest Annual Return and subsequent Forms No. 288 notifying changes in officers. There are severe penalties on both the company and its directors for late submission of the Annual Return, because it is so necessary to satisfying the requirement that information about the company be made public.

The Registrar of Companies

The Registrar of Companies is charged with the maintenance of records of documents filed by companies, in accordance with the requirements of the Companies Acts.

The address is:

The Registrar of Companies
Companies House
Crown Way
Maindy
Cardiff CF4 3UZ
Tel: 0222 388588

or:

The Registrar of Companies
Companies House
55 - 71 City Road
London EC1Y 1BB
Tel: 071 253 9393

Companies House is open to the public from 9.00 am to 5.00 pm Monday to Friday (excluding public holidays) in both Cardiff and London. The latest time to make application for a company search is 3.00 pm.

Insolvency

Insolvency legislation is to be found in:
- The Insolvency Act 1986
- The Company Directors Disqualification Act 1986
- Delegated legislation, including the Insolvency Rules.

There are three ways to wind up (that is, close) a company:
- Members' voluntary liquidation
- Creditors' voluntary liquidation
- Compulsory liquidation.

The Insolvency Act makes provision for other 'rescue' procedures:
- Administration
- Receivership
- Corporate voluntary arrangements.

Voluntary liquidations

Where the company is solvent, and the voluntary liquidation is initiated by the shareholders, it is known as a members' voluntary liquidation; if the company is insolvent, it is a creditors' voluntary liquidation.

In a creditors' voluntary liquidation, 75 per cent of the shareholders at a meeting must vote in favour; they then appoint a liquidator. A meeting of creditors must be held within 14 days, at which the creditors may reject the liquidator appointed by the shareholders in favour of one of their own appointment, as well as a liquidation committee of up to five creditors or shareholders.

The liquidator will realise the company's assets and use them to pay (in this order):
- The expenses of the liquidation (including his/her own liabilities and any tax arising from the liquidation)
- Creditors whose debts are secured by a fixed charge
- Liquidator's fees
- Preferential creditors (mainly taxes and employee claims)
- Creditors whose debts are secured by a floating charge
- Unsecured creditors
- Shareholders.

Compulsory liquidations

The process of compulsory liquidation is usually begun by a creditor who has not been paid and makes a petition to the Courts (usually, the High Court). The Court, if it accepts the petition, appoints a liquidator (usually the Official Receiver, a civil servant) who may call a meeting of the creditors to confirm their acceptance of his appointment or to appoint another liquidator.

Where court delays might prejudice the company's position in liquidation, a provisional liquidator may be appointed.

Receivers

Receivers are appointed on the basis of a contract between the company and a lender, under which the lender has the right to do so if the company is in default of its obligations. The Insolvency Act 1986 regulates the actions of receivers.

The contract will normally give the lender a fixed or floating charge over certain company assets. If specified conditions occur (loan repayments are not made on time, for example), the charge 'crystallises' and the loan becomes due in full immediately. A receiver is appointed; his/her job is to ensure that the loan is repaid to the lender.

The receiver manages the business on behalf of the company, with power to realise assets, enforce contracts in the company's name, but with no responsibility for pre-receivership liabilities or contracts.

The order of priority of payments by the receiver is:

- Liabilities entered into by him
- Receiver's fees
- Amounts due to creditors secured by fixed charges out of the proceeds of the assets on which the charges are secured
- Preferential creditors (taxes and employee claims) out of assets secured by floating charges
- Amounts due to creditors secured by floating charges out of the remaining assets thus secured.

Any surplus is released to the company (represented by the directors), or a liquidator, if one has been appointed, in which case it is available for the unsecured creditors.

Unsecured creditors are not involved in a receivership, though they have rights of information from the receiver. They also have the right to petition the courts for the appointment of a liquidator. If their petition is granted, the liquidator will examine the validity of the debenture under which the receiver has been appointed and deal with any surplus from the receivership.

Administration

Administration is a legal shield against creditor action while arrangements for the reconstruction or reorganisation of the company are agreed. The directors, the company itself or any creditor may apply to the courts (usually, the High Court) for an administration order.

The presentation of the petition for an order acts to suspend payments to creditors and protects the company from legal proceedings, including winding up and execution against its goods.

Until the administration order is lifted, the administrator manages the company's affairs as agent of the company, with powers similar to those of a receiver. He has three months to prepare proposals to put to a meeting of creditors. At this meeting, a majority by value of those voting and a majority of those to whom notice was sent (excluding those connected with the company) must approve the proposals, which may include a voluntary arrangement.

Arrangements with creditors

Schemes of arrangement with creditors may be approved by the courts but rarely are because of the time delay involved. Instead, voluntary arrangements are used. These require only the approval of the company's shareholders and creditors.

The approval of shareholders is secured through a simple majority of those voting. Creditors' approval requires a 75 per cent majority of those voting and a majority by value of those to whom notice was sent (excluding those connected with the company).

Disqualification of directors

A director of an insolvent company may be held personally liable for the company's debts and disqualified from further holding office as director in other companies, if he allows a company to continue trading when he knew or ought to have known that there was no reasonable prospect of the company avoiding insolvent liquidation.

Other legal topics

Journalists working in the financial area may find it useful to have some knowledge of the law relating to contracts, employment, trade unions, banks, building societies and friendly societies, consumerism, competition and mergers, as well as the environment, though these topics are beyond the immediate scope of this book. In addition, an appreciation of how EC law impacts on national law could be helpful.

Financial accounting and reporting

Financial accounting and reporting in the UK has, historically, been governed by enacted legislation, influenced in recent years by Directives on company law issued by the European Community. It is the Companies Act 1985, as amended by the Companies Act 1989 and by various Statutory Instruments, which forms today's primary legislation on the preparation of company accounts.

This legislation puts the onus on directors *inter alia* to:

- Maintain proper accounting records
- Provide shareholders with annual financial statements that 'comply with applicable accounting standards' and present 'a true and fair view of the state of affairs of the company as at the end of its financial year and of its results for the year'
- Ensure, where a company has subsidiaries, that its financial statements include the financial position and results of those subsidiaries, in order to provide consolidated group accounts.

There is a popular misconception that the auditors (who are required by law to report to shareholders on the annual financial statements) are also responsible for the preparation of these statements. The law makes it clear that they are the directors' financial statements, and that the responsibility of the auditors is to provide an independent opinion to shareholders as to whether the accounts presented are 'true and fair', and prepared in accordance with applicable accounting standards and in conformity with the requirements of the Companies Act.

The legislation prescribes the form and minimum content of company accounts, but allows adaptation of the form to meet the special nature of a company's business. Companies within a legal definition of small or medium-sized may take advantage of an exemption from certain disclosure requirements.

UK and non-UK companies whose securities are listed on The Stock Exchange ('listed companies') are required to comply with rules, known as the Continuing Obligations, which include requirements for the content of annual reports and accounts in addition to the Companies Acts requirements.

Accounting standards

While the Companies Act includes basic rules regarding accounting policies to be used in companies' financial statements, the 'applicable accounting standards' referred to in the law are essentially outside the legislation. They comprise:

- Statements of Standard Accounting Practice (SSAPs), which were issued by the Accounting Standards Committee (ASC) of the Consultative Committee of Accountancy Bodies (CCAB). The ASC ceased on 31 July 1990; 19 SSAPs, however, currently remain authoritative (numbered 1 to 25 except 6, 7, 10, 11, 14 and 16, which have either been withdrawn or superseded)
- Financial Reporting Standards (FRSs), issued by the Accounting Standards Board (ASB), which assumed responsibility for setting UK accounting standards in August 1990. The ASB's activities are supervised by the Financial Reporting Council, whose members are drawn from industry, academia and the accounting profession
- Consensus views of the ASB's Urgent Issues Task Force (UITF), which was established in 1991 to provide mandatory guidance where unsatisfactory or conflicting interpretations have developed or seem likely to develop in areas where an accounting standard or Companies Act provision exists.

Before an FRS is issued, the proposed accounting treatment is issued for comment as a Financial Reporting Exposure Draft (FRED); often, proposals are floated earlier in a discussion draft.

While FRSs deal with accounting issues of general application, industry groupings such as the Oil and Gas Federation provide guidance on specific accounting issues appropriate to their members. These Statements of Recommended Practice (SORPs) (which currently cover such topics as pension funds, charities, accounting in the oil industry, insurance companies and banks), do not form part of 'applicable accounting standards' referred to in legislation. They are, in effect, voluntary guidance, but implementation of the accounting treatments suggested therein is generally encouraged and is an influencing factor in 'market acceptability' of financial statements for companies within those industry sectors.

The Financial Reporting Review Panel

The Financial Reporting Review Panel (FRRP) is a sister body to the Accounting Standards Board, under the control of the Financial Reporting Council. It is not a standard-setting body; rather, its remit is to investigate cases of reported non-compliance with legislation or accounting standards in the preparation of public companies' financial statements. It has the power to apply to the courts for an order requiring a company to withdraw or modify its published accounts.

It has a chairman, deputy chairman and 21 members. As cases arise, working groups of five or more of the FRRP's members meet to consider them.

Accounting principles

UK company law requires a company's annual financial statements to be drawn up using the 'historical cost convention', which effectively means that transactions are recorded in the books, and therefore in the financial statements, at the cost to the company on the date that the transaction took place.

A few exceptions are allowed – tangible fixed assets (for example, land and buildings) and intangible fixed assets (such as patents) used in the business, and investments held for the long term, may be included at market values (and, in practice, many companies do this); assets that are traded in carrying out the business, such as investments and stocks, may be included at current cost, although this is relatively rare in practice.

The impact of this mixture of historical cost and valuation bases makes the UK balance sheet somewhat difficult to interpret, as discussed further below. It also means that some care must be exercised when looking at a company's results for a period, particularly in inflationary times. For example:

- The profit recognised by company A on the sale of stock that it acquired two years ago is likely to be significantly higher than that recognised by company B on the sale of similar stock acquired in the last month. However, the cost of replacing that stock, at today's values will be the same for both companies
- The annual charge for depreciation (wearing out) for a building bought ten years ago will be less for company A, which accounts for that building at historical cost, than for company B, which records that building at a higher revalued amount – say, market value two years ago.

The accounting bases used by a company (historical cost or valuation of tangible fixed assets is only one example of these) must be reflected in the notes to the company's annual financial statements and, in particular (although not exclusively), in the 'statement of accounting policies', which usually forms one of the first notes to the financial statements.

This statement of accounting policies reflects:

- Those policies which, even if prescribed by law or accounting standards, are fundamental to an understanding of the accounts
- Those policies that the particular company has chosen from alternatives available to it from the law or accounting standards (or where standards do not exist)
- Policies that the company has chosen to adopt, despite the requirements of law or accounting standards, because, in the opinion of the directors, the prescribed policies would not result in the accounts showing a true and fair view.

It cannot, therefore, be overemphasised that a study of the accounting policies, and of the other notes to the accounts, is as important as – and perhaps even more important than – reading the primary financial statements themselves.

Despite this apparent range of 'choices' of accounting policy, there are four fundamental concepts that underlie all companies' financial statements:

- Going concern: That an enterprise will continue in operational existence for the foreseeable future, so that its financial statements assume no intention to liquidate or curtail its scale of operations
- Accruals: That income and costs are recognised as they are earned or incurred and matched with one another to the extent possible within the profit and loss account of the period to which they relate, subject to the prevailing effect of:
- Prudence: That income should not be anticipated and that provision should be made for known liabilities, whether the amount is known with certainty or as a best estimate in the light of available information
- Consistency: Of accounting treatment of like items within and between accounting periods.

If a company chooses to change an accounting policy, or is forced so to do because a new accounting standard or an UITF consensus is issued, **and** if the effect of the change of policy is material, the effect of that change is reflected by a 'prior year adjustment' in the comparative figures. The results for the current year are calculated entirely in accordance with the new policy, and retained profits brought forward are adjusted as if the new policy had always been in effect. The fact that such a prior year adjustment has been made must be spelt out in the notes to the accounts.

The only other instance where a prior year adjustment arises is where there has been a fundamental error in the previous year's accounts; again, this should be obvious from a reading of the notes to the financial statements.

The annual financial statements

Companies' annual financial statements comprise:

- A profit and loss account, for the company standing alone **or**, if it has subsidiaries, on a group consolidated basis
- A statement of total recognised gains and losses, which deals with those gains and losses not recognised in the profit and loss account
- Balance sheets, for the company standing alone **and**, if appropriate, on a group consolidated basis
- A statement of company, **or**, if appropriate, group consolidated, cash flows
- Suitable notes that, as required by law or accounting standard, amplify relevant figures in the primary financial statements above.

Further information on the requirements for the primary financial statements and notes is given later in this chapter. Comparative (prior year) figures are almost always required to be given.

In addition, a Directors' Report is required to be annexed to the financial statements. This is required by law to include:

- A statement of the group's activities and any significant changes
- A fair review of developments in the business during the year and of the financial position at the end of the year
- Particulars of important events since the year end
- An indication of likely future developments in the business
- Details of directors' interests in the share and loan capital of companies in the group, and of directors' share options.

In practice, some companies choose to confine the information in the directors' report to the absolute legal minimum; others use the directors' report or an 'Operating and Financial Review' to provide a full narrative explanation of events during and since the year under report. The ASB published a framework for a voluntary 'Operating and Financial Review' in July 1993 which may lead to a significant enhancement of the explanatory narrative given by the directors annexed to the annual financial statements of all major UK companies.

Returning to the financial statements themselves, it is important to remember that:

- Financial accounting and reporting is, to a large extent, an 'art' rather than a science; whilst the law and accounting standards prescribe certain basic accounting concepts and policies, these cannot deal with the many practical problems of judgement and estimation required of directors in preparing financial statements
- The legislative requirement for financial statements to be prepared for the members of the company (the shareholders) has been explained and amplified in case law in terms of their original, central and primary purpose being to assist the members in an informed appraisal of the stewardship effected by the company's directors. The information given therein may, of course, be of assistance to other users of the financial statements but the relevant estimates and judgements are made primarily in the context of providing information to existing shareholders
- The information is, essentially, a historical record of past achievement. Much has been said about the predictive nature of the information given in company's financial statements; predictive judgements, based on the information given, are, however, 'in the eye of the beholder' and therefore necessarily highly subjective.

Companies do, of course, publish financial information other than that included in their annual financial statements. Listed companies, for example, are required by the Yellow Book to publish unaudited 'interim accounts' – a half-yearly financial announcement that, under current regulations, is only required to include a group profit and loss account. It has been suggested that the regulations might be amended so that interim announcements include also a group balance sheet and a group cash flow statement; the question of auditing interim accounts has also been raised.

Listed companies are also obliged to inform the market of their full year's results, by publishing unaudited preliminary figures as soon as these are known – often four to six weeks before the full annual report is published. Other Stock Exchange regulations require financial information to be included in prospectuses or circulars issued to shareholders.

Such financial information for listed companies is governed by the regulations in the Yellow Book which, for UK companies, requires UK accounting standards to be followed. The information given is, however, generally less than that prescribed for companies' annual financial statements, and a warning to that effect always accompanies such financial information. The same warning accompanies any general financial information published by all companies, so that readers are aware whether or not they are looking at the annual financial statements required by the Companies Act.

Cash flow statements

Probably the easiest of the primary statements to understand, this statement shows the group's cash inflows and outflows. Take care, however; cash inflows may arise in one part of the group and outflows in another, so that cash resources may not be as well-matched as appears from the financial statements.

The format of the cash flow statement is prescribed by the ASB's first standard, FRS 1, which requires a group to show its cash flows under standard headings according to the activity that gave rise to them:

- Operating activities
- Returns on investments and servicing of finance (dividends and interest)
- Taxation
- Investing activities (sales or purchases of those major assets used in the business or investments held for the long term)
- Financing (proceeds from new issues of shares or loans taken out, or share redemptions or loan repayments).

The statement 'balances off' to a movement on 'cash and cash equivalents', the latter defined as short term, highly liquid investments that are readily convertible into known amounts of cash without notice and which were within three months of maturity when acquired, less advances from banks repayable within three months from the date of advance.

FRS 1 also prescribes certain 'cash flow footnotes' that must be given, including:

- A reconciliation between 'cash flow from operating activities' and the operating profit shown in the profit and loss account
- Major changes in the group's financing, not arising from cash flows – the acquisition of a major asset by way of a finance lease, for example.

GROUP CASH FLOW STATEMENT

	£m	£m
Net cash inflow from operating activities	65.7	68.6
Returns on investment and servicing of finance		
Interest received	2.1	1.3
Interest paid	(33.5)	(10.9)
Dividends received from associated undertaking	7.6	4.9
Dividends paid	(32.6)	(27.9)
Net cash outflow from returns on investment and servicing of finance	(56.4)	(32.6)
Taxation		
UK Corporation taxation paid	(26.4)	(26.7)
Overseas taxation paid	(6.4)	(4.2)
Taxation paid	(32.8)	(30.9)
Investing activities		
Purchase of tangible fixed assets	(51.4)	(34.2)
Purchase of subsidiary undertakings	(176.2)	–
Sale of tangible fixed assets	86.8	21.2
Acquisition related provisions utilised	(8.1)	–
Net cash outflow from investing activities	(148.9)	(13.0)
Net cash outflow before financing	(172.4)	(7.9)
Financing		
New debenture loan stock	200.0	–
New short-term loans	19.3	23.2
Repayment of amounts borrowed	(28.4)	(11.6)
Net cash inflow from financing	190.9	11.6
Increase in cash and cash equivalents	**18.5**	**3.7**

Profit and loss account

The profit and loss account aims to show the results arising from the group's trading during the year (and the cost of any related financing). It therefore includes transactions that may not necessarily be settled in cash until the following year; similarly, it may include transactions settled in cash in the preceding year but not taking effect until the current financial period. For example:

- A company buys stock in year 1 and sells it in year 2. It does not record as an expense the stock it purchases in year 1; rather, and so long as it expects an overall profit to be realised, it 'carries that cost forward' and records the expense in the profit and loss account of year 2, at the same time recording the trading income, so as to measure the profit on the transaction in its profit and loss account in year 2
- The company makes a sale in year 2, but does not collect the cash until year 3. The sale is, however, an event of year 2; the company therefore records the sale in year 2, so long as it can reasonably expect the cash to be realised
- A company's year end is December. It takes out a new insurance policy and pays the premium for one year in advance on 1 October. In its profit and loss account for that year, it records only one quarter of the premium cost; it defers the cost of the other nine months, to be charged in the profit and loss account in the second year.

The above examples provide some indication of the 'accruals concept' mentioned earlier, and an insight into some of the simpler areas of judgement exercised in preparing financial statements.

The format of the profit and loss account, and the detail of information that must be disclosed in footnotes thereto, is prescribed in law and accounting standards.

In FRS 3 *Reporting Financial Performance*, the ASB requires that all components of operating profit should be analysed between continuing operations, acquisitions and discontinued operations – to highlight, *inter alia*, the extent to which readers of the accounts may expect earning streams to continue in the future, and the extent to which a growth in earnings has been achieved organically or by acquisition.

Equally, these particular areas of profit and loss are, if material, required to be separately disclosed immediately after operating profit:

- Profit and losses on the sale or termination of an operation
- Costs of a fundamental reorganisation
- Profits or losses on the disposal of fixed assets.

The tax implications of these three items are required to be detailed in a footnote to the financial statements.

GROUP PROFIT AND LOSS ACCOUNT

	£m	£m
Turnover	1,266.2	921.4
Cost of sales	(869.1)	(617.1)
Gross profit	397.1	304.3
Distribution costs	(36.8)	(31.6)
Administrative expenses	(193.0)	(135.8)
Operating profit	167.3	136.9
Income from interests in associated undertakings	7.6	4.9
Net interest payable	(31.4)	(9.6)
Profit on ordinary activities before taxation	143.5	132.2
Taxation	(42.0)	(41.6)
Profit on ordinary activities after taxation	101.5	90.6
Minority interest	(5.5)	(4.8)
Profit for the financial year	96.0	85.8
Dividends	(34.8)	(30.9)
Amount transferred to reserves	**61.2**	**54.9**

It is worth pointing out that, in the UK, the profit before taxation shown in the profit and loss account is not that on which taxation is charged. A number of adjustments are made in a separate tax computation, to determine taxable profit. In addition, of course, a group profit and loss account may include profits from overseas territories where the tax rate differs substantially from that in the UK.

Major variations between the effective tax rate shown in the financial statements and the fiscal corporation tax rate should be ascertainable from the notes to the accounts. The segmental analysis of pre-tax profit will indicate whether there are major overseas earnings; the 'taxation footnote' should indicate whether the tax charge has been significantly influenced by losses brought forward or by significant 'taxation allowances'.

It is worth noting two frequent phenomena:

- The impact of deferred taxation: Where the impact of taxation allowances is to reduce tax payable in one year but effectively only defers payment of that tax to the relatively near future, a company must set up in its accounts a liability for the tax thus deferred. The tax charge in the accounts will then include both current tax (that is, giving rise to an imminent cash payment) and deferred tax (likely to give rise to a cash payment in the next few years)
- Advance Corporation Tax (ACT): This tax is payable whenever a UK company pays a dividend; it may, however, be recouped against future corporation tax payable, where sufficient levels of UK corporation tax are likely to be paid. For accounting purposes, if it seems unlikely that significant levels of UK corporation tax will be payable, the 'irrecoverable' ACT must be written off within the tax charge in the profit and loss account. This tends to give rise to a 'lumpy' tax charge, particularly for those groups paying UK dividends but where a major part of earnings (and thus tax payable thereon) arises overseas.

Perhaps the most over-used number associated with the profit and loss account is that of earnings per share. Calculated as 'earnings after deducting minority interests in subsidiary profits and dividends paid to preference shareholders, divided by the average number of shares in issue during the year', it is over-quoted as a measurement of success or failure of a company. It cannot be emphasised too frequently that the true measure of a company's performance can only be gauged by critical review of **all** the figures in the profit and loss account and, of course, the extent to which those profits have been turned into cash, as reflected in the cash flow statement.

Statement of total recognised gains and losses

In FRS 3, the ASB requires a new primary statement of 'total recognised gains and losses' to be provided. An adjunct to the profit and loss account, this new statement is designed to highlight any gains and losses made by a group in the year **not** reflected in the group profit and loss account. Such gains and losses are, by law and accounting standards, carried directly to reserves and have always been visible in the notes to the accounts. The new primary financial statement, however, is intended to highlight these effects, of which the most notable examples are:

- Gains or losses arising on re-translating the net resources of overseas subsidiaries from the exchange rate used in the prior year to that currently applicable
- The unrealised surpluses or deficits arising from revaluing to current market value long term assets used in the business.

Transactions with shareholders (such as dividends paid) are excluded from this statement.

STATEMENT OF TOTAL RECOGNISED GAINS AND LOSSES

	£m	£m
Profit for the financial year	96.0	85.8
Unrealised surplus on revaluation of properties	24.2	2.8
Total gains and losses for the year before currency adjustments	120.2	88.6
Currency translation differences on foreign currency net investments	(3.6)	2.2
Total recognised gains and losses	**116.6**	**90.8**

Balance sheet

The Companies Act 1985 sets out a very prescriptive format for the balance sheet, which is probably the most misunderstood of the primary financial statements. While the profit and loss account summarises activities for a year, the balance sheet presents only a 'snap shot' of the group's financial position at the end of the year. The relative significance of the assets and liabilities set out in the balance sheet can, therefore, vary considerably for a seasonal business, depending on its accounting date.

For example, the balance sheet of a tour operator at the beginning of its holiday season (having taken payment from holiday makers, but not settled airline and hotel supplier accounts) will be 'cash rich' – certainly more so than the position at the end of the season. The volume of stock shown in the September balance sheet of a fireworks manufacturer is likely to be very different from that in the December balance sheet.

Moreover, and perhaps most importantly, the emphasis on historical cost accounting means that the balance sheet is **not** a statement of a company's value. With the exception of certain industries (property investment, for example, where the vast majority of assets are revalued to market value at each year end), the balance sheet does not, and cannot be expected to, demonstrate in any way the value of a group. Under current accounting practice (and with the exception of those items valued at market value), it simply acts as a 'repository' of those items of cash income or expenditure that have not yet been credited or charged in the profit and loss account.

The terms used in the balance sheet are:

- Fixed assets: These are defined in law as the assets intended for use on a continuing basis in the company's activities. Tangible fixed assets include such items as property, plant and equipment; intangible fixed assets include goodwill (where it has not been written off), brands, patents and trademarks. Fixed asset investments are those held for the long term, from which a group does not expect to generate dealing profits, but which are held for their income earning capacity
- Current assets: Essentially, 'all other assets', the term current does not infer a likelihood of short term realisation as cash. Indeed, companies may hold within current assets such long term items as maturing whisky stock and credit sales that may only be realisable by instalments over several years. In reviewing a set of accounts, reference to the footnotes to ascertain the presence of such long term items – and an understanding of the business in which the company operates – is essential to an appreciation of the relative liquidity of the items held as current assets

GROUP BALANCE SHEET

	£m	£m
Fixed assets		
Tangible assets	574.9	525.4
Investments	93.2	88.9
	668.1	614.3
Current assets		
Stocks	367.2	247.9
Debtors	328.3	229.2
Investments	5.0	5.8
Cash at bank and in hand	37.8	1.0
	738.3	483.9
Creditors		
Amounts falling due within one year	(456.8)	(353.4)
Net current assets	281.5	130.5
Total assets less current liabilities	949.6	744.8
Creditors		
Amounts falling due after more than one year	(222.0)	(72.3)
Provisions for liabilities and charges	(32.9)	(2.9)
Net assets	**694.7**	**669.6**
Capital and reserves		
Called up share capital	92.0	41.0
Share premium account	12.5	12.5
Revaluation reserve	183.3	159.1
Profit and loss account	381.7	433.2
	669.5	645.8
Minority interests	25.2	23.8
	694.7	**669.6**

- Liabilities (or creditors): In contrast to assets, the categorisation of liabilities (as either due within one year, or due after one year) reflects the time scale within which the group's obligations are due for settlement. A further category, 'provisions for liabilities and charges', includes those items whose nature is rather more vague; they are obligations which the group has incurred or is certain to incur, although at the current time the amount of such obligations or the date on which they will arise cannot necessarily be ascertained with certainty
- Shareholders' funds: These include not only capital subscribed by shareholders but also realised profits retained within the business (as retained profit and loss account) and unrealised gains (such as revaluation reserves)
- Minority interests: The cumulative profits attributable to minority shareholders of subsidiary undertakings.

The net figure of assets minus liabilities should equal the total of shareholders' funds and minority shareholders' interests – otherwise the balance sheet does not balance! But be careful! Some balance sheet formats (as allowed in law) present a total of fixed assets plus current assets minus current liabilities, and match this with a total of long term liabilities, shareholders' funds and minority interests. In these cases, the reader of the accounts is required to do a little arithmetic, in order to work out what net assets are.

A combination of law and accounting standards prescribes the policies to be followed for various items on the balance sheet – for example:

- Tangible fixed assets: Initially accounted for either at cost or market value, tangible fixed assets are required to be depreciated, so that the profit and loss account suffers a charge for 'wearing out' over the useful economic life of the assets concerned. The rates of such write down must be detailed in a note to the financial statements. In the exceptional cases where a permanent impairment in the value of fixed assets is identified, a supplementary write down must be made to their balance sheet value
- Stocks: Stock-in-trade must be carried in the balance sheet at the lower of cost or net realisable value, and thus provision is made against carrying value, at the time that it is foreseen that a loss may be realised when the stock is eventually sold.

The notes to the financial statements are required, by law and accounting standards, to provide analysis and explanation of many of the items on the balance sheet. A reader of the accounts should look carefully at the notes, when trying to understand the figures given in the primary statements.

Group accounts

If a company's financial statements are intended to demonstrate the directors' stewardship of the company during the financial year, then a logical extension of this, where a company controls other companies, is to include the controlled resources within the financial statements. Group consolidated accounts are a mechanism for doing this – but they are an imperfect mechanism, and should be treated with care.

A group's cash resources, for example, as shown in its balance sheet, may include cash held in an overseas subsidiary – and not available to the parent company, because of exchange control restrictions. The profits shown in a group profit and loss account may not be available to the shareholders of the parent company, either because an overseas company is not allowed, by local law, to remit those profits to the UK or because, if they were to remit a dividend, penal rates of withholding tax would be demanded by the local tax authority. The only profits that one can be sure are available to pay future dividends to parent company shareholders are those in the **parent company** balance sheet – and even then, allowance may have to be made for any irrecoverable UK Advance Corporation Tax on such dividends. What then is the purpose of group accounts? They provide an indication of the total resources managed by the directors of the parent company which may, of course, be quite properly retained in subsidiary companies to develop those businesses. They are, for now, the only picture, albeit imperfect, of the whole group – and at least the law demands that, when all the individual accounts are added together to show 'the group picture', common accounting policies are applied within the group.

It is the Companies Act 1989 amendments to the Companies Act 1985, coupled with guidance from the ASB (FRS 2, in particular), which prescribes those 'subsidiary undertakings' whose accounts must be consolidated with those of the parent company. The term 'subsidiary undertaking' applies to companies, partnerships and unincorporated associations in which the parent controls a majority of the voting rights or controls a majority of the directors' votes. Additionally, subsidiary undertakings include **any** entities in which the parent has an actual or future share interest, which it holds for the long term, and where:

- The parent company actually exercises a dominant influence over the subsidiary undertaking
- The parent and subsidiary undertaking are managed on a unified basis.

The only effective exceptions to these rules are where the parent's ability to control the subsidiary undertaking is very short term or is severely restricted.

The accounts of 'subsidiary undertakings' are fully consolidated with (that is, added to) those of the parent. Even if the parent does not control 100% of the subsidiary undertaking, the group financial statements still include 100% of its results and balance sheet. The share of net profit attributable to minority shareholders of the subsidiary for the year is removed from the profit and loss account in a 'minority interests' line, and the cumulative impact shown separately on the balance sheet.

There is another category of entity, 'associated undertakings', whose results and resources are also shown in group accounts, but not fully consolidated. Associated undertakings are those in which the group has an investment, held for the purposes of securing a long-term contribution to its activities by the exercise of control or influence, and where it actually exercises a 'significant influence' over the undertaking's operating and financial policy.

An associated undertaking is therefore not controlled to the same extent as the subsidiary undertaking, although the group does take a part in its management. The group's share of the results of an associated undertaking is brought into the group profit and loss account in a single line entry, and its share of the tax charge is reflected within the group tax charge (although separately disclosed in the notes to the accounts).

The cumulative share of net assets of the associated undertaking is shown as a one line item on the group balance sheet (often within 'fixed assets – investments'), matched by an entry in the group's cumulative reserves. There is, unsurprisingly, currently some debate whether group reserves should be 'bolstered' by such an entry, since the group may not be able to enforce the associated undertaking to distribute its earnings.

Business combinations

Accounting for an existing group is difficult enough; accounting for the point at which a new company joins a group has been the subject of considerable controversy – and the debate continues.

Accounting for a 'business combination' may take one of two forms:

- Merger accounting: Relatively rare (because its application is restricted by the law), under which the financial statements of the 'new group' are presented on the basis that it had always existed – that is, the profit and loss accounts and balance sheets of the merging companies are merely added together for both the current and prior years
- Acquisition accounting: Most commonly used, where the resources of the new subsidiary are incorporated into the group accounts at their 'fair values' at the date of acquisition, and the group accounts include the profit of the subsidiary with effect from that date only. No adjustment is therefore made to prior year financial statements.

Two interesting questions arise with respect to acquisition accounting. The first is the extent to which the 'fair value adjustments' made with regard to the new subsidiary should include provisions for reorganisation costs and trading losses expected during a period of rationalisation. The issue is that, because such provisions are effectively made 'before acquisition' and profits for the new subsidiary only incorporated from the time of acquisition, these costs are excluded from the group profit and loss account. Indications are that, in future, the creation of acquisition provisions will be considerably restricted.

The second is that of goodwill. A parent company that pays (that is, gives up a resource of) £3 million to buy a new company, and, on an acquisition accounting basis, brings the resources of that new subsidiary into its accounts at a fair value of £2 million, has paid the 'missing' £1 million for goodwill. That goodwill payment represents what the purchaser is willing to pay for the intangible benefits associated with the business – for example, market share, good management, stable workforce, branded products, etc, or, in some cases, a control premium. Such benefits are undoubtedly assets, but their nature is hard to define and, moreover, they are difficult to value on an ongoing basis – that is, unless a 'willing buyer' and 'willing seller' have agreed a price in a purchase and sale transaction. Under existing UK accounting practice, the goodwill paid on acquisition (that is, the £1 million in the example above) is most commonly written off straight away against reserves in the group accounts, which does not appear to reflect the economic reality of the transaction.

New standards from the ASB on both fair value accounting and goodwill are expected in 1994.

Future issues

Reference has already been made to the current debate surrounding fair value acquisition accounting, accounting for goodwill and accounting for associated undertakings. Considerable thought is also being given to such issues as:

- Off-balance sheet finance: How to account for those transactions whose legal form differs from their economic substance, with the implication that 'legalistic accounting' could result in an enterprise's assets and finances not being fairly reflected in its balance sheet. Proposals set out in an Exposure Draft (FRED 4) are likely to become a new FRS by the end of 1993
- Capital structures: Whether the law or accounting standards currently provide sufficient guidance as to whether particular forms of financing should be classified as liabilities or

shareholders' funds; and whether improved guidance can be given to preparers of accounts on reflecting costs of finance in their periodic profit and loss accounts. New guidance proposed in FRED 3 is likely to become an accounting standard by the end of 1993
- Related party transactions: Whether, and to what extent, groups should disclose the nature of related party transactions and their impact on their financial performance.

As indicated earlier, accounting and financial reporting is to a large extent an art rather than a science; 'rulebooks' will never deal with the many practical problems involved in drawing up corporate entity financial statements. Nevertheless, it seems clear, that as corporate structures become ever more complex, and the financial community invents ever more complicated financial instruments, the accounting standard setters will have to work very hard to maintain the standard of financial reporting of which the UK has long been proud.

Auditing

As noted earlier, annual financial statements of all active UK incorporated companies are currently, by law, required to be audited. Thus, once the directors of the company have prepared a draft of the financial statements, an external and independent auditor is required to give his opinion to shareholders as to whether the accounts presented are 'true and fair' and in accordance with applicable accounting standards and with the requirements of the Companies Act.

The auditors are also required by law to reach an opinion whether:
- Proper books and records have been kept by the company
- As auditors, they received the information and explanations they required to carry out their work
- The financial statements are in accordance with the books and records
- The directors have, in the financial statements, given the disclosures of directors' emoluments and directors' transactions required by the law
- The information given in the directors' report is consistent with the financial statements.

The auditors do not give specific report on the above five matters, unless problems are encountered; the absence of any specific comment on these matters in the auditor's report is therefore a confirmation of satisfaction.

Only 'Registered Auditors' are permitted by law to give such independent auditor opinion on companies' financial statements. Registration is given by one of the auditing 'Self Regulatory Organisations' (SROs):

- The Association of Authorised Public Accountants (AAPA)
- The Chartered Association of Certified Accountants (ACCA)
- The Institute of Chartered Accountants in England and Wales (ICAEW)
- The Institute of Chartered Accountants in Ireland (ICAI)
- The Institute of Chartered Accountants of Scotland (ICAS).

Registration as an auditor requires not only that one holds a professional qualification from one of these bodies but also that one complies with of regulations concerning on-going training, technical expertise, organisation and quality control. Adherence to these required standards is checked by the Joint Monitoring Unit (for ICAEW, ICAS and ICAI members) or the Monitoring Unit (for ACCA and AAPA members), which pay periodic visits to auditing firms to monitor the standards applied.

The actual work of the auditor is governed by Statements of Auditing Standards, issued by the Auditing Practices Board (funded and controlled by the Consultative Committee of Accountancy Bodies, including the bodies referred to above, with the exception of the AAPA) and by its predecessor body, the Auditing Practices Committee. These statements comprise a mixture of mandatory procedures and suggested guidance.

City institutions

The City is often referred to as the 'Square Mile', a misnomer that is becoming ever more incorrect as the City spreads both within London and beyond its boundaries. Institutions, forced out by the rising cost of office space, have begun to move to other locations, principally Docklands.

Bank of England

At the core of the City is the Bank of England, the UK's Central Bank, established in 1694. The Bank:

- Advises government on monetary policy and implements economic policy through its intervention in the markets
- Has a key role in determining base interest rates and influences the exchange value of sterling
- Is responsible for the licensing and supervision of all banks operating in the UK
- Regulates some of the financial markets, such as those for gilt-edged stock, and the wholesale markets in sterling, foreign exchange and gold
- Keeps the government's bank accounts, raises money for the government and issues bank notes and coins
- Acts as banker to the commercial banks and holds the country's gold reserves.

When founded, the Bank of England was a commercial bank with private shareholders, though it acted as banker to the government, arranged government borrowings and issued bank notes in England and Wales (it acquired the monopoly to issue bank notes in the Bank Charter Act, 1844). In 1946, the Bank was nationalised, having for many years previously behaved more as a public institution than as a commercial bank.

The Bank's customers include:

- 10,600 private account-holders, mainly staff and pensioners
- The commercial banks, which settle accounts among themselves daily through their accounts at the Bank of England and keep an agreed amount (currently 0.4 per cent of their sterling deposit base, called 'cash ratio deposits') with the Bank

- Foreign central banks, which keep accounts in order to be able to transact foreign exchange and bullion business in London
- The government – its main banking accounts for receipts of taxes and payments of social welfare, defence and other spending are kept with the Bank.

The Bank advises government on monetary policy, though it is the Treasury that takes the final decisions. Policy is implemented by the Bank's intervention in the market. Since it is the final provider of liquidity to the system through its dealings with the discount houses, the Bank can choose the rate at which it provides funds each day. This rate then influences the commercial banks' own base rates.

The UK's gold and foreign exchange reserves are held at the Bank of England in an Exchange Equalisation Account. This was set up in the 1930s, after Britain left the gold standard, to check undue fluctuations in the external value of sterling. Through this account, the Bank buys sterling in exchange for foreign currencies when it wants to curb a fall in the value of sterling or sells sterling when it wants to curb a rise.

Supervision

The Banking Act, 1979 gave the Bank of England power to authorise and supervise all deposit-taking institutions, except building societies which are supervised by the Building Societies Commission. The Act, which was updated and strengthened in 1987, provides that deposit-taking institutions must gain prior approval of the Bank before commencing business and must submit to continued supervision of their activities by the Bank.

To become and remain authorised, an institution must show:

- Adequate capital
- Adequate liquidity
- Fit and proper management
- Adequate internal systems and controls to enable management to assess their risks properly and to ensure that prudent banking procedures are observed.

In the event of a bank failure, depositors are entitled to limited compensation from a Deposit Protection Fund, set up and administered by the Bank and financed by contributions from all the banks (of which there are about 550 in London, more than half being branches or subsidiaries of foreign banks).

The Bank's Banking Department operates the clearing function for settlement of inter-bank claims; in addition, the Central Gilts Office and Central Money Markets Office services provide paperless settlement facilities.

The Bank is the sole issuer of currency notes in England and Wales (Scottish and Northern Irish banks issue their own notes and coin is issued by the Royal Mint, on behalf of the Treasury). The notes are designed and printed at the Bank's own printing works and issued mainly through the commercial banks. The Bank's branches (in Bristol, Birmingham, Leeds, Manchester and Newcastle) also distribute new notes and take in old notes for sorting and reissue or destruction.

Governance

A Governor, Deputy Governor, and 16 other members of the Court of Directors are appointed by the Crown (to serve for five years in the case of the Governor, and four years in the case of the directors). Up to four of the Directors may serve as executives of the Bank and a number of Associate Directors, with the same status as executive directors, have been appointed in recent years. The Bank's staff numbers some 5,000.

Clearing banks

The term 'clearing bank' has its origins in the banks' practice of clearing cheques and settling accounts with each other at the end of each working day. In the past, this had to be done through the Bankers' Clearing House, a limited company owned by the banks that constituted the Committee of London Clearing Bankers (CLCB). However, as building societies and insurance companies developed their services in the early 1980s, the need for an expanded system arose whereby financial institutions other than banks could operate a daily clearing system. This led to the establishment of the Committee of London and Scottish Bankers (CLSB), on 1 December 1985, which replaced CLCB as the trade association for the eight major banks (Bank of Scotland, Barclays, Lloyds, Midland, NatWest, The Royal Bank of Scotland, Standard Chartered and TSB).

On 31 March 1991, the British Bankers' Association assumed responsibility for the work carried out by CLSB, which ceased to exist on this date.

The basic functions of the clearing banks are to accept deposits and lend to those who wish to borrow and provide payment services such as cheques and credit transfers.

Often the term 'clearing bank' is used loosely to mean any of the Big Four (Barclays, Lloyds, Midland and NatWest), possibly as these are the oldest, dating back to the early nineteenth century when legislation caused the Bank of England to lose its monopoly. However there are many other banks, British and foreign, as well as other financial institutions, now involved in the clearing system. This has come as a result of the huge growth in the financial services industry in recent years, with even department stores issuing their own credit cards and selling loans. The banks have had to modernise their approach to the customer as they face new competition in the market place.

An example of this competition can be seen in the building societies flooding of the market with interest bearing cheque accounts in 1987 as a fight back against the banks' provision of home loans. Though not a bank, Abbey National is today the U.K.'s third biggest banking institution.

The British Bankers' Association

The British Bankers' Association (BBA) is a trade organisation representing 325 banking institutions, including all the major banks. The association's membership is made up of UK banks and overseas banks that have branches in the UK.

Essential for membership is authorisation under the Banking Act, 1987, which stipulates issued capital and undistributable reserves amounting to not less than £5m and entitlement to use a banking name (there are restrictions on the use of the word 'Bank' in a company name – see section on Company formation in the chapter on *Company Law*). Foreign banks must be authorised to use a banking name in their home country.

The BBA's role is to monitor and express the industry's views on domestic and international developments to the appropriate bodies – for example, Parliament, particular ministers, the Bank of England, European Community institutions and the media. This includes commenting on new legislative and regulatory initiatives and raising concerns about existing arrangements. To do this, the BBA maintains strong links with other trade associations, academics, professional firms and plays a full part in the workings of the European Banking Federation.

The BBA also functions as an information resource for its members, through newsletters and circulars. In the passage of the Finance Bill in 1990, the BBA was a valuable link between parliament and the media and, as a result, aims to continue to raise its profile nationally.

The BBA's secretariat includes specialists in tax, accounting, legal matters, consumer and public affairs, banking supervision and investment matters.

APACS

In 1985, the Association of Payment Clearing Services (APACS) began operations. APACS is the independent body responsible for the structuring and development of the clearing system, which includes money transmissions and payment clearing activities. Membership comprises all those financial institutions providing such services in the

UK. APACS is the umbrella organisation for the three clearing companies that operate the clearing system. These are:

- Cheque & Credit Clearing Co. Ltd
- CHAPS & Town Clearing Co. Ltd
- BACS Ltd.

Cheque & Credit Clearing Co. Ltd

Cheque & Credit Clearing Co. Ltd deals with high volume paper clearing. The company operates two bulk paper clearings that are situated in London, the Cheque Clearing and the Credit Clearing. Most inter-bank cheques (except the small number of high value cheques) go through the first clearing. Credit Clearing handles paper credit items.

In 1990, 2,293 million cheques and 174 million paper credits with a total value of £1,198 billion passed through the clearings. Inter-member settlements are made at the end of a three-day clearing cycle through members' accounts at the Bank of England.

CHAPS & Town Clearing Co. Ltd

CHAPS & Town Clearing Co. Ltd operates two high-value same-day clearings in the UK. Clearing House Automated Payment System (CHAPS) provides a same-day guaranteed sterling electronic credit transfer service within the UK. Since January 1992, the system allows for payments of £1,000 or more (previously, £5,000 was the minimum accepted). Payments are transmitted from branch to branch via a computer system.

Town Clearing handles low volume debit paper clearing for cheques and other items of £500,000 or more. Only items drawn on and paid into branches of member banks in a limited area in the City of London can use the system.

In 1990, 90 per cent of the two companies' transactions went through CHAPS. The aggregate value of the 9 million transactions was £23,656 billion.

BACS Ltd

BACS Ltd was established in 1971 as the Bankers Automated Clearing Services, and renamed Bulk Electronic Clearing in 1986 when it became part of the APACS structure. BACS provides an automated clearing house service in the UK for transactions originated by either the settlement members or others sponsored by them to use the service, of which there are currently 50,000 providers. The payments processed by BACS are direct debits, automated credits and standing orders.

BACS processed 1,602 million transactions in 1991 valued at £667.5 billion, broken down between direct debits (53 per cent), automated credits (32 per cent) and standing orders (15 per cent). Settlement is made across members' accounts at the Bank of England at the end of a three-day processing cycle.

Currently, there are 21 members of APACS and all are members of one or more clearing companies. Other financial institutions and banks can become members of APACS provided they meet the relevant criteria. During 1991, APACS, the BBA and the Building Societies Association put together a code of banking practice, setting out for the first time the rights and duties of banks vis-à-vis their personal customers. Copies of this code are available free from the BBA (see *Directory* for address).

Merchant banks

One of the major activities of merchant banks nowadays is corporate finance. They act as advisers to companies involved in take-overs and mergers, and to those wishing to raise money whether direct from lenders or via The Stock Exchange.

Merchant banks in London have their origins in the last century. When London was emerging as a major international trading centre, it was the merchant banks which financed trade.

A merchant bank, usually owned and run by a single wealthy family, lent the credit of its name, for a fee, on bills of exchange drawn on them by traders needing credit. This practice was known as accepting bills of exchange, which lead to the name 'Acceptance House'. Later, large successful traders provided the capital for merchant banks to finance other activities such as investing in overseas development projects, laying the foundations for foreign government and industrial loans from the London capital market. Trade in bills of exchange became so profitable that foreign houses set up offices in London to reap the profits available there.

International trade is today financed through the major market currencies and bills of exchange no longer have the same market force. The financing aspect of the early merchant banks' business evolved to become the primary activity they are concerned with today.

The main activities of merchant banks in the area of corporate finance are:

- Advising companies on investments
- Securities trading, both as brokers and market makers: Merchant banks can be involved by sponsoring capital issues on behalf of customers, ensuring the total capital is underwritten by other financial institutions or buying the customer's total share issue themselves and selling it further to subscribers
- Advising on take-overs and mergers: This developed in the 1950s and 1960s when the banks acted as advisors. Their role today involves identifying the best avenue for their client company in a take-over or merger situation, either share

transfer (shares in one company are exchanged for shares in a newly formed company), share buyout (buying out the old shareholders) or share control (a company acquires in excess of 50 per cent – often as little in excess as 50.1 per cent – to have control of the target company)
- Fund management, increasingly serving corporate and government clients and a small number of individuals in portfolio management, with the aim of maximising profits and minimising tax liability
- Foreign business, where merchant banks continue to lead the field in terms of international expertise in commodities and markets and operate on a world-wide scale for their customers
- Finance, providing medium term (two to five years) and long term loans (more than five years) as a capital injection or venture capital, under terms negotiated between the bank and the borrower.

To meet the regulatory requirements that certain activities must be conducted by separate companies, most merchant banks are today conglomerate groups. Even so most still manage to offer a wide range of services.

There is no exact equivalent of a merchant bank outside London. The closest is what is called 'investment banking' in the United States.

In comparison to the high-street banks, merchant banks are small and none employs more than a few thousand people. Because of the large amount of capital needed in this type of banking, many of the merchant banks in the City are either owned by one of the big banks or by a large corporation.

Foreign banks

A foreign bank is one that has its headquarters outside the UK and has one or more branches operating in London or elsewhere in Britain. Currently there are 450 foreign banks in the UK from 73 different countries, employing about 35,000 staff.

Foreign banks were first attracted to London at the end of the last century by the wide range of facilities available there, namely insurance, trade finance and shipping. Many institutions closed during the two world wars but reopened in peacetime.

These banks kept large working balances of sterling in their London branches to finance international trade through the acceptance business (see Merchant banks) and for funding loans for overseas borrowers.

When the Eurodollar market developed in the 1960s (when investors with dollars invested outside the US balked at reinvesting them in the US at the then low interest rates), a large number of American banks opened branches in London (they are now the largest group of foreign banks). The Eurodollar business now dominates London's foreign currency banking business and foreign banks have succeeded in obtaining most of this. They also offer a full range of international banking services including investment advice and finance for international operations.

With the suspension of exchange control, foreign banks have made aggressive inroads in the domestic market. They offer lower interest rates than their clearing bank competitors as they can finance themselves from the wholesale money markets, as opposed to depending on raising capital through their branch networks, at high cost.

Factors that make London an attractive centre for foreign banks are:

- Few controls
- An orderly market
- Economic and political stability
- Well educated and hard working staff
- Central time zone
- English is the primary international business language
- Advanced communications systems
- Major international markets in insurance, shipping, Stock Exchange, foreign exchange, commodities
- Innovative solutions/updating of systems, for example the London International Financial Futures Exchange (LIFFE).

Insurance companies

An insurance policy is a contract designed to protect the policy holder against financial loss sustained as a result of some specific event, such as an accident, a death, damage to property or theft.

One can distinguish:

- Tangible financial loss, where the insurance company pays the value of the items insured at the time of loss (except in the case of domestic appliances and household goods where the original value may be taken into account)
- Intangible financial loss such as health/life, where the policy holder determines a value by the policy he/she chooses.

As the nature and needs of these two types of policies differ greatly, insurance can be categorised as either general or long term. The law requires the two types of business to be conducted separately, which is problematic for companies engaged in both but necessary as the distinction has significant implications on the way risk is dealt with.

Taking motor insurance as an example of general insurance, companies aim to take in enough in premiums from individual policies over a twelve month period to exceed the estimated total output on claims plus overheads during that time and allow for profit. How the insurance company manages the inflow capital determines its profitability as, frequently, claims can exceed initial estimates. Sound investment of the premium capital during the year brings in additional income, which is often sufficient to turn an underwriting loss (premiums less claims) into an overall profit.

In the case of life assurance, policies are long term and so premiums cannot be altered from year to year, though indexation clauses are now common. This offers the possibility for long term investment and emphasises the importance of estimating the value of likely claims from year to year, the costs of which determine the premiums on new policies.

In both types of insurance, risk reduction is involved through the aggregation of independent events, analysis of events in each area of insurance determining the rates at which contracts will be offered to cover the specifics of that area. This minimises the risk for the company. By making investments that correspond to the time scale of its liabilities, the insurance company can increase potential profitability for that period.

There are four main aspects of insurance today:

- Personal insurance: Life, accident, health
- Property insurance: Household, car, aeroplane, small boats, livestock
- Liability insurance: Usually to cover third party risks, for example public and professional liability, employers' liability
- Contingency insurance: To cover events that could cause financial loss, for example loss of profits, insurance of debts.

The insurance business is regulated by the Insurance Companies Act, 1974, amended in 1981 and the Insurance Brokers' Registration Act, 1977 which states that only the following may carry on insurance business:

- A body authorised to do so by the Secretary of State under the Insurance Companies Act, 1981
- A body previously authorised under the Insurance Companies Act, 1974
- A member of Lloyds'
- A registered Friendly Society
- A trade union or employers' association, in relation to the provision for its members of provident benefits or strike benefits
- A bank carrying on the business of credit insurance, suretyship and similar cover against financial loss.

The Insurance Companies Act, 1981 classifies the business into long-term and general as follows:

- Long-term: All life and annuity business, contracts of insurance to provide sums of money on marriage or birth, linked long-term business, permanent health insurance, and pension fund management contracts.
- General: Under the Act, there are 17 classes – Accident, aircraft, aircraft liability, credit insurance, damage to property, fire and natural forces, general liability, goods in transit, legal expenses, miscellaneous financial loss, motor vehicle liability, railway rolling stock, ships, ships' liability, sicknesses, suretyship and vehicles.

Regulations are issued from time to time under the Acts to cover areas such as:

- Contents of advertisements
- Fraudulent inducements to do business
- Conduct of brokers
- Rights of insurers
- Rules regarding valuation and provision of information to the insured
- Allocation of funds to policy holders
- Duties of company directors in regard to informing the Secretary of State about management changes or changes in company structure
- Publication of annual statements and the deposit of accounts with the Secretary of State and the latter's powers of intervention.

Besides insurance companies, banks and other financial institutions operate in the insurance market but the most influential institution in the market, responsible for much of the development of the business, is Lloyds'.

Lloyds'

Lloyds' of London, the world's best known insurance market, traces its origins back to the 17th century and Edward Lloyds' coffee house. Merchants met there and, among other business, bought and sold insurance cover, primarily for ships and cargoes.

Lloyds' now has its own purpose built and distinctive steel-clad building, with 30,000 members grouped in some 400 syndicates. The affairs of each syndicate are managed by an underwriting agent who is responsible for appointing a professional underwriter for each main class of business.

Governance

The Council of Lloyds' was established under the Lloyds' Act, 1982, and has overall responsibility for and control of the affairs of Lloyds'. It consists of:

- Twelve working members of Lloyds'
- Eight external members
- Eight nominated persons.

The Council elects its Chairman and two deputy chairmen from among its working members; one of the nominated Council members holds the third position of Deputy Chairman and salaried Chief Executive.

The Council is responsible for:

- The management and superintendence of the affairs of Lloyds'
- The regulation and direction of the business of insurance at Lloyds'
- The election of new underwriting members
- The review of requirements for underwriting membership
- The rules governing financial security, to which all members must adhere.

The 12 working Council members form the Committee of Lloyds' which deals with the day-to-day workings of the market.

Membership

Although its surroundings have altered, little has changed in the basic operation of the market for insurance. Lloyds' still has no shareholders; it is a society of underwriters, all of whom accept insurance risks for their personal profit or loss and are liable to the full extent of their personal wealth to meet their insurance commitments.

The publication, 'Membership: The Issues', a guide to prospective members, states:

- Insurance is a risk business and therefore both profits and losses can be made
- Underwriting is a cyclical business and membership should be viewed as a long term venture
- Membership is personal – it cannot be shared, sold, transferred, assigned or bequeathed
- A member is currently required to prove that he has wealth of £250,000 which must be maintained at all times
- The entire personal wealth of a member, and not only the means he has shown, is at risk
- The member takes no part in the day-to-day underwriting but must delegate the complete control of his affairs to his underwriting agents

- A member is required to lodge funds at Lloyds', related to his premium income limit
- A member will assume both assets and liabilities in respect of business underwritten before he joined the syndicate
- Cash calls on members may be made immediately on commencement of membership but no underwriting profits may be paid out before the end of the third year of membership
- A member (or his estate) remains liable for losses until his Lloyds' affairs are wound up after the underwriting year has been closed out.

Agents

There are different types of agent operating in the Lloyds' market:

- Members' agent: Manages a member's affairs but does not conduct underwriting
- Co-ordinating agent: Where a member has more than one members' agent acting for him, one will be appointed to co-ordinate his Lloyds' affairs
- Managing agent: Runs one or more syndicates.

The ownership, control, and activities of Lloyds' agents are regulated by Council.

The rules include:

- Continuing tests of fitness and propriety
- A requirement that the active underwriter of the syndicate and at least 2 directors/partners of a managing agent participate in the syndicate(s) managed by them
- A ban on Lloyds' brokers or their directors/partners having any interest in a managing agent or vice versa
- Rules designed to address and minimise conflicts of interest
- Effective systems for monitoring premium income
- Regulation of reporting by managing agents, with requirements for the preparation of syndicate annual reports.

Underwriting

Lloyds' underwriters have no contact with the public; all their business comes through Lloyds' brokers, of whom there are some 250. A broker's duty is to negotiate the best possible terms for his client, placing the risk at Lloyds', an insurance company, or both.

When a broker receives a request for insurance cover, he will make out a 'slip' – a sheet of folded paper with the details of the risk. He then negotiates a premium with underwriters specialising in that type of business – marine, non-marine, aviation, motor, or new technology – perhaps obtaining several quotations. When the broker is satisfied that he has the best rate for the risk, the leading underwriter, having set the rate, will take a proportion of the risk on behalf of his syndicate. Armed with this 'lead', the broker approaches as many other syndicates as necessary to get the slip fully subscribed – that is, get the risk fully covered.

Both broker and underwriter operate on the basis of 'utmost good faith'. That is, the underwriter's signature on a slip is absolutely binding – in honour, if not in law – and the broker can be confident that a valid claim would be settled, even if it were presented before a policy had been issued; on the other hand, the underwriter knows that the broker will have disclosed all material facts about the risk accurately and fairly.

Lloyds' Policy Signing Office
After a policy has been prepared by the broker from details on the fully subscribed slip, it is checked, signed and sealed by Lloyds' Policy Signing Office (LPSO) on behalf of the syndicates concerned. Settlement of amounts for premiums and claims between brokers and syndicates is made centrally each month on agreed figures issued by LPSO.

The Stock Exchange

The Stock Exchange is a market where company shares, options on shares and government securities are traded. Approximately 7,000 UK and foreign company shares are listed on the exchange but it is in government stocks that the major trading, by volume, takes place – about 70 per cent of turnover.

The Stock Exchange exists to fulfil two market functions:

- The primary market provides a mechanism for companies listed on the exchange to raise long term capital through the issue of securities
- The secondary market provides liquidity for investors through dealing facilities in the shares of companies listed on the exchange.

The primary fund-raising market is the most important because without it, there would be no need for the second; but it is the second that generates most of the activity of The Stock Exchange.

A Stock Exchange listing
A company that wishes to be listed on The Stock Exchange (that is, have its shares traded on the exchange) must:

- Display a three year trading record
- Provide a full-scale accountants' report on its prospectus
- Make available 25 per cent of its shares to the public
- Have a sponsor.

A sponsor is usually a merchant bank or firm of stockbrokers and is expected to:

- Prepare the prospectus for sale
- Scrutinise the accuracy of the information given in the prospectus to ensure its overall fairness
- Obtain Stock Exchange approval
- Ensure that the marketing of the company's shares is carried out in a manner consistent with an orderly market
- Satisfy themselves that the directors could provide all the information necessary for a market in the company's shares, could be expected to honour their obligations to the shareholders and creditors, and understand the responsibilities associated with office in a publicly quoted company.

Independent 'reporting accountants' are engaged by the sponsor to:

- Prepare a 'long form' report on the company, covering its history, trading activities, management structure and financial position
- Prepare a 'short form' report for inclusion in the prospectus
- Report on the company's profit forecast
- Ensure that all taxation clearances have been obtained by the company and, where appropriate, its shareholders.

The Stock Exchange requirements for companies seeking a market quotation are set out in *The Listing Rules* (from September 1993, previously *Admission of Securities to Listing*), otherwise known as 'The Yellow Book'.

'Big Bang'

The Stock Exchange was completely transformed by 'Big Bang', the name given to the changes that took place in 1986. It has, it can be argued, also been changed by the crash that took place, two years later, in October 1988.

Big Bang arose through the insistence of the Office of Fair Trading that the fixed commissions scheme operated by The Stock Exchange, which maintained the distinction between 'jobber' and 'broker', was anti-competitive and thereby pushed up costs for investors. In particular, the OFT was concerned on behalf of small investors and planned to take legal action against The Stock Exchange. The then Secretary for State for Trade and Industry, Cecil Parkinson, intervened; as a result, the OFT case was dropped in return for the removal of The Stock Exchange's fixed commissions.

Fixed commissions maintained the jobber/broker split because brokers, with no means of competing on price, had no incentive to deal on their own account.

Variable commissions meant that prices quoted to investors varied. And as brokers were attracted to hold 'easy' stocks for their own account, jobbers saw their markets being eroded and moved to deal direct with investors. Thus was born dual capacity, under which a firm could be both jobber and broker – principal and agent.

Other pressures that served to hasten Big Bang included:

- The internationalisation of corporate fund-raising
- The ability to trade via telecommunications links in international markets without the need for a physical market-place
- The challenge to the expensive UK dealing system from New York brokers (Stamp duty was charged at 2 per cent on all transactions in the UK until March 1984, when it was reduced to 1 per cent, still giving an advantage to US brokers; at present, the rate depends on the type and type of transactions but it is likely that stamp duty on share transactions will be abolished in 1994).

Jobbers had also found that their capital base was, by and large, too small. Mergers had reduced the numbers of jobbing firms from over 400 in 1920 to 17 in 1985, only five of which were of any size. Capital availability depended on the partners' pockets, either to introduce fresh capital or to forego earnings in favour of reinvestment. The range of stocks had become too great for any one firm to carry a decent holding in each listed stock and so jobbers specialised, to the extent that as few as two firms might deal in the shares of a particular company – hardly the makings of a 'perfect' market.

The introduction of capital from outside investors was a major benefit of Big Bang, as far as the City was concerned. Not only could individual partners cash in their years of service and investment in their firm (and many did) but fresh funding could be raised to allow the firm to compete more aggressively in the new market-place.

The financial institutions that had hitherto been banned from the City – in particular, overseas financial institutions that had trading bases in London in order to participate in the Eurobond/Eurodollar market – took to the changes with gusto. Major capital injections were made overnight; partners retired with small (and some large) fortunes; those in the 'marzipan layer' (that is, the managers, who lay just below the 'icing' of partners) began an ever-speeding game of musical chairs as individuals and teams moved from institution to institution in search of spiralling salary and performance related bonus packages; and market capacity grew beyond even the most optimistic hopes of achievable volumes.

It took 12 to 15 months for the market to realise that it was hopelessly overextended. By that time, the seeds of the October 1988 crash had been sown. But when it came, few were truly prepared. Many small investors, bitten by the privatisation 'bug' and convinced that investing in shares was an effortless and riskless way of making money, were badly caught out. It was fortuitous that the privatisation issues occurred at a time when the extra capacity in the market required a massive widening of the circle of investors but the market took false hope from the surge to buy privatisation stocks and did not do enough to prepare for the inevitable fall.

Gilts

On the gilts (Government securities) side, significant changes also took place as a result of Big Bang.

Prior to 1986, all gilts were sold into the market by the government stockbroker, the senior partner of the firm of Mullens & Co. He sold on the stock to the two jobbing firms, Akroyd & Smithers and Wedd Durlacher Mordaunt, which between them controlled 85 per cent of the market. They, in turn, sold on the stock to the specialist brokers who bought on behalf of their clients.

Post Big Bang, the government stockbroker joined the staff of the Bank of England and applications were sought for the positions of primary gilt dealers – 29 were received, though two later dropped out. Each became a market maker, buying and selling and holding stocks on its own account as well as for clients.

How did 27 expect to make a living where only two did so before? Whatever the initial expectations, the reality was that only a handful could last in the gilts market. The end of 1987 saw a stream of erstwhile gilts market makers retiring, bruised and bloody.

Computerisation

The other major change that came with Big Bang was computerised trading. Though not part of the process of deregulation itself, it was essential for the operation of the deregulated market-place.

Trading on The Stock Exchange had always been on an 'open outcry' basis. Jobbers and brokers had their positions on The Stock Exchange floor (in those hexagonal boxes one sees in interior pictures of The Stock Exchange building) and moved back and forth between them, making deals. When the market was active, the origin of the term 'open outcry' became clear – trading took place in conditions of apparent bedlam! But in times of increasing volumes of transactions, and thus increasing paperwork, automation was the only way to hold down costs.

Now all trading is done on computer. Market makers quote their prices on The Stock Exchange Automated Quotation system (SEAQ) and deals can be settled directly through it. Prices are also displayed on TOPIC screens which give quotations only and do not permit trading.

TOPIC

TOPIC is the comprehensive financial information service provided by The Stock Exchange. It includes:

- A mid-price trend service on over 2,000 UK equities and gilt-edged securities
- The SEAQ Market Maker competing quote service
- The SEAQ International competing quote service
- Real time prices from international financial markets
- Company announcements as they are issued
- Dealing prices from the London Traded Options Market
- LIFFE prices
- Closed User Group services
- FOREX foreign exchange services live from major banks.

The system uses Videotex technology to transmit information from The Stock Exchange's computers to the user's TOPIC terminal. Alternatively, the user may receive TOPIC on any IBM compatible PC, using special software. Heavy users of TOPIC may arrange for a computer-to-computer link, using TOPICLINE, and distribute the information internally on networks, reducing the need for dedicated terminals.

CNS, the Company News Service, publishes company announcements on TOPIC as they are received, including:

- Disclosures relating to take-over and merger situations
- Suspension and restoration notices
- Forthcoming board meetings
- New issue notices
- Index to certain Stock Exchange Council notices.

CNS is available in edited or full text versions. The basic edited service is free to TOPIC users; full text involves an additional fee.

Companyfile, launched in May 1989, is another TOPIC service, providing up-to-date reference information on listed companies and their activities.

Other services available on TOPIC include:

- Fixed interest market information
- Gilt-edged market turnover
- Economic and financial service (Balance of Payments, Exchange Rates, Gross Domestic Product, Money Supply and Retail Prices)
- Information from the Bank of England and HM Treasury.

RNS, the Regulatory News Service, was launched in late 1990 and provides a computer-readable feed of all listed and USM company announcements. Companies are allowed to provide their own summaries of complex or lengthy documents that go out over RNS.

SEAQ

The Stock Exchange Automated Quotations System (SEAQ) is at the heart of the changes that have affected the City, post-Big Bang.

It provides the means whereby dealing can occur off the floor of the exchange (while still being subject to regulation, of course). It forms an interface between market makers and their customers, allowing the entry and display of 'bid' and 'ask' prices on the SEAQ system. Market makers use their dealer terminals to enter two-way prices for the SEAQ stocks in which they are registered and to report their trades. From the information entered by market makers, best bid and ask prices and last trade information (for 'alpha' stocks only) are displayed on the TOPIC service. Market makers must display their two-way prices throughout a Mandatory Quote Period, approximating to the trading hours of the market to which the prices relate.

Subscribers to SEAQ or TOPIC see up-to-the-minute market prices on their screens.

Changes that came into effect on 14 January 1991 have led to the reclassification of listed stocks – as alpha, beta, and gamma, though these differ from earlier classifications with the same names (see section on Classification of shares in the chapter on *Investments*) – and a new method of deciding on the publication of prices of stocks on SEAQ.

Now, a Normal Market Size (NMS) is calculated for each stock. This is based on the £value of customer turnover in the past 12 months divided by the closing mid-price on the last of the quarter multiplied by 10,000. This gives an average trading quantity for the stock. Twelve bands of NMS, ranging from 500 to 200,000 shares have been set. Shares with an NMS of 2,000 or more (the shares of about 900 companies) will have immediate publication on SEAQ of all trades up to 3 times their NMS; deals above this size will be published after a 90 minute delay. Previously, only 191 alpha stocks were thus published.

Trades in shares with an NMS of 500 or 1,000 will not be published on SEAQ but will appear in the next day's Daily Official List.

SAEF

SAEF, the SEAQ Automatic Execution Facility, enables dealers to enter orders to trade directly via their terminals. These orders are automatically executed by SAEF, ensuring the best price to investors. All trades in up to 10 per cent of each stock's NMS are eligible for execution through SAEF, which went live in February 1989.

It provides the following advantages:

- Brokers can execute small orders without having to telephone a market maker for prices
- Computer readable output from SEAQ can be used to prepare contract notes
- An 'audit trail' to track a particular deal

- A guarantee that a deal has been transacted at the best possible price available at the time
- Instant exposure of market prices.

SEAQ International

SEAQ International provides a market service for some 700 international securities traded on the International Equity Market in London. In addition, it disseminates London market prices for these securities around the world, through commercial quote vendor services, including:

- Bridge
- Market Eye
- NASDAQ
- Pont Data
- Quick
- Quotron
- Reuters
- Telekurs
- Telerate.

TAURUS

TAURUS was the name given to the computerised settlement system that The Stock Exchange planned to introduce to automate the transfer of company shares in a manner similar to money transfers in the banking system. It was planned to eliminate the bulk of the paper from what is currently a predominantly paper-driven clerical process, by transferring and settling shares electronically. It was intended to complement the electronic trading systems available under SEAQ and reduce delays between execution of a trade and on line confirmation.

However, after many delays, the TAURUS project finally collapsed in 1993. It was too ambitious, too costly, and did not achieve the time savings that were its *raison d'être*. It has now been replaced by a new less ambitious system developed by a task force set up by the Bank of England.

The key elements of the new system are:

- It will provide 10-day rolling settlement by July 1994
- It will provide five-day rolling settlement by January 1995 (though private investors will be free to negotiate a different settlement period with their broker)
- An electronic transfer system, called CREST, will be operational by 1996. This will be a transfer mechanism for equity trades, allowing electronic payment and receipt of stock. Participants will have the option of a totally paperless procedure or of receiving share certificates

- Membership of CREST will be open to institutional investors, brokers, registrars and custodians, who will have to meet certain minimum criteria
- CREST will have the capacity to handle dividends, rights issues and proxy voting in conjunction with registrars
- A bank (probably the Bank of England) will be at the centre of the payments system, to hold accounts for each of the settlement banks
- The Bank of England intends to admit only banks that are part of the Clearing House Automated Payments Systems (CHAPS).

The Bank of England's involvement in the new system is taken in the market as a good indication that CREST will succeed.

Governance

The Stock Exchange is an unincorporated body established by deed. Its members elect a Board (prior to July 1991, a Council), which is responsible for the organisation and administration of the exchange; the Rules of The Stock Exchange govern the behaviour of members. Under the terms of the Financial Services Act, 1986, members of The Stock Exchange are deemed to be carrying on investment business and so are required to be authorised. Their self-regulating organisation is The Securities and Futures Authority (previously, The Securities Association).

The Board comprises:

- The chairman, chief executive, chief financial officer and up to three members of the executive management team
- (As non-executives) two senior investors; two chairmen of chief executives of listed companies; one banker; 15 representatives of various parts of the securities industry.

The new board is responsible for long term strategy and overseeing the formation and execution of policy.

To become a member of the Stock Exchange involves buying a 'seat' on the Exchange. At one time, the price of seats was within the reach of individuals; now only large corporations can afford the amounts involved.

International aspects

The Stock Exchange's international aspects include:

- Through Big Bang, overseas financial institutions previously excluded from membership of the exchange were permitted to become members, thus increasing both membership and market capacity

- Through SEAQ, a visible market is available to investors around the world
- In November 1986, The Stock Exchange merged with the International Securities Regulatory Organisation to create the world's first truly international stock exchange
- Under the Financial Services Act, the concept of Recognised Investment Exchanges (RIEs) was introduced. These need not be in the UK, provided their rules of business – in particular, in relation to investor protection – are at least equal to The Stock Exchange's rules. There are now 27 overseas exchanges (ORIEs) recognised by The Stock Exchange.

In addition, to meet the opportunities of an integrated Europe, the Federation of Stock Exchanges in the EC has entered into a number of co-operative ventures:

- A jointly owned price and information dissemination system
- A proposal to list the major European companies on all the exchanges of the Federation simultaneously
- A proposal to create a European wholesale or professional market for international equities trading.

The Unlisted Securities Market

The Unlisted Securities Market, or USM as it is more commonly known, was established in 1980 to provide a market in which companies could raise capital without the expense of a full listing on The Stock Exchange. A second objective was to provide a source of liquidity for the investors in the shares of such companies, which would make the shares themselves more attractive. The final objective was to bring transactions that took place in the shares of non-listed companies within the ambit of The Stock Exchange, where previously they would have remained outside the market and regulatory mechanism except for those cleared under the then Rule 163(2).

However, despite its vigorous growth to date, the USM is still a young and often volatile market, with the narrowness of public holdings of some stocks causing sudden and violent price fluctuations.

To qualify for entry to the USM, a company:

- Need only display a three year trading record, instead of the five year record required for a full Stock Exchange listing
- May provide a shortened version of the full-scale accountants' report on a prospectus
- Need only make available ten per cent of its shares to the public (This can be most important to control conscious entrepreneurs).

Investing on the USM is riskier than on The Stock Exchange. Typically, compared to companies listed on The Stock Exchange, USM companies will be:

- Smaller
- At an earlier stage of development
- Achieving dramatic growth rates in the early years that cannot be sustained in the medium term (turnover that doubles each year will have increased 32-fold after five years and more than 1000-fold after ten)
- Usually dependent on technological innovations for their success and at risk from further developments by others in the same area of technology
- Closely linked with the founder(s).

In addition, investment on this market suffers from a lower level of liquidity than the main market, with shares closely held and dealing margins wide as a result.

The Traded Options Market

The Traded Options Market is a market within The Stock Exchange. Shares in 70 or so companies are traded, as well as contracts on gilts, currency and the FT Index.

Options are the right to trade in a security at a given price (the 'exercise price') within a specified period (before the 'expiry date'). Traded options go one stage further and are negotiable securities themselves.

Traded options come in 'classes' and are available for three expiry dates and at a range of exercise prices. A contract comprises 1000 shares, though prices are quoted per share.

Cash deals are the order of the day, with payment being required within 24 hours of the transaction.

For an example of how options are used, see the chapter on *Investments*.

Commodities markets

Commodities are basic substances such as coffee, sugar, cocoa, rubber, wool or cotton (soft commodities) or some form of mineral, such as silver, tin, lead, copper or zinc. A commodity market can only exist in homogenous substances that will not change and therefore can be sold by sample. A wide range of commodities is traded in the USA, including items such as plywood and frozen pork bellies.

Because of the volatility of prices following good or bad harvests, markets developed where commodities could not only be bought and sold but also could be 'bought forward' (that is, a price paid now for delivery at a future date). The price paid for the commodities 'future' depended on the expectations of future availability. Some purchasers never actually took delivery of the commodity on the due date but sold their right to do so (the future contract) before the delivery date. Thus the futures markets were born.

Modern commodities markets have more to do with dealing in the rights in products than dealing in the products themselves. Commodity markets have the advantages of:

- Being international, with consequent benefits for liquidity
- Having low dealing costs
- Providing trading opportunities both when the market is rising and when it is falling
- Dealing in real assets, providing security of some sort if all goes wrong.

The Royal Exchange, where the commodities markets operate in London, was opened by Queen Victoria in 1844 (the first purpose-built market opened in 1571) and is located near the Tower of London. The building was not used as an exchange from 1928 until the London International Financial Futures Market moved into it in 1982.

The main London commodities markets are:

- The London Commodity Exchange
- The London Metal Exchange
- The International Commodities Clearing House.

The London Commodity Exchange

Soft commodities – cocoa, coffee, sugar, wool, rubber, grain – are traded on the London Commodity Exchange (LCE). Each commodity has its own market association of traders which deals with market rules, contract specifications and settlement of disputes. For example, The Coffee Terminal Market Association of London Ltd, The Gafta Soyabean Meal Futures Association and The United Terminal Sugar Market Association are members of LCE. These associations, known as TMAs, ensure that there is close conformity between the futures market and physical trade.

In 1986, the LCE became the London Futures and Options Exchange (FOX) until July 1993, when it reverted to its original name.

The London Metal Exchange

The London Metal Exchange (LME) has operated in London for the past 100 years, trading in non-ferrous metals: aluminium, copper, lead, nickel, silver, tin, zinc.

The exchange has 30 members and is managed by a Committee of Subscribers who are elected by the members. Subscribers can be individuals on their own accounts or representatives of institutions.

The LME is a self-regulatory international exchange trading in futures and physical commodities. Trading takes place through what is known as a 'ring', comprising producers, consumers, brokers and merchants, all of whom are members of the exchange. Each member trades as a principal and carries responsibility for their market obligations. Metals are stored in the Exchange's registered warehouses and are moved to meet contract agreements.

The International Commodities Clearing House
This is an independent institution owned by various clearing banks and run separately. This is where all contracts traded on the floor of the LCE and LME are cleared and settled. Contracts must also be registered and guaranteed by the ICCH. Therefore, all members of the TMAs must also be members of the ICCH. If both parties in the contract are members of ICCH, there is no need for either to put up funds to guarantee performance on the contract.

The London International Financial Futures Exchange

LIFFE was formed from the merger in March 1992 of the London International Financial Futures Exchange (first founded in September 1982) and the London Traded Options Market. It is Europe's leading financial futures and options exchange and the third largest in the world.

Financial futures are a derivation of commodity futures. From commodities, the markets moved to exchange rates futures, having identified the potential in the floating rates of exchange between currencies that characterised the 1970s. Later, interest rate futures were added.

One of the major financial futures contracts is based on the movement of the FT-SE 100 index. This relatively new index is constructed from the share prices of 100 top shares, making it almost as good an indicator of market performance as the older FT Actuaries All Shares Index. However, because the FT-SE 100 is recalculated minute by minute during Stock Exchange trading hours, it is literally an up-to-the-minute market indicator. This contract operates much like traded options, except that instead of an underlying security there is an index.

Other financial futures contracts – in short term interest rates, UK, US and German government bonds – are used to protect against exchange risk or interest rate risk, as appropriate. Major users are the financial institutions and multinational companies. The former tend to be speculators and the latter, hedgers. Hedgers tend to lock in to either a lending or a borrowing rate.

LIFFE provides facilities for dealing in futures contracts in:

- Short term interest rates
- Government bonds
- Stock indices
- Foreign currencies.

In addition, LIFFE offers traded options in financial instruments and currencies.

Each contract is defined as to:

- Standard quantity – for example, $1 million
- Specific financial instrument – both the type and its quality in terms of coupon rate and maturity
- Delivery date
- Initial margin
- Trading hours.

Trading on LIFFE is 'on margin' – that is, the investor only puts up part of the full price of the contract, effectively trading largely on credit. Because of this it is possible to make large profits on a small investment; equally, it is possible to lose heavily and quickly.

Although trading on the floor of LIFFE is by open outcry, it is backed by massive technological support. The exchange can accommodate 3,000 traders and has 4,000 telephone lines relaying orders and information to 1,000 display terminals.

LIFFE's clearing house clears transactions between traders. It effectively removes credit risk, by ensuring that all transactions are made with the clearing house rather than individual traders. Traders deposit cash or collateral 'on margin' which safeguards the clearing house's risk.

Automated Pit Trading (APT) was introduced in November 1989, using technology to present pit trading on screen. It was followed by Automated Trading and Order Matching (ATOM), which together with APT, provides a single automated trading system.

The Baltic Exchange

The Baltic Exchange, which was bombed by terrorists in mid-1992, is the world's leading shipping market, matching ships with cargoes and vice versa.

The exchange dates back to the last century. Merchants found it convenient to meet at the exchange to do business, because of the proximity of trade credit and marine insurance in the City. And, as Britain had built and operated the world's largest merchant fleet, London was the natural place for the freight market to develop.

The exchange's full name is the Baltic Mercantile and Shipping Exchange. The mercantile aspect relates to dealings in commodities, such as grain, oil, soya, seeds, potatoes, fats and meats. The shipping side of the exchange is a market for vessel chartering, cargo space and second-hand ships. Since 1949, the exchange has also operated a market for air chartering.

The London Gold Market

The London Gold Market consists of five member firms dealing in gold bullion. One of the member firms also melts, processes, refines and assays gold.

The firms meet twice daily in the offices of NM Rothschild for the fixing of the London gold price and to absorb new gold or other gold offered at the fixing. The members sit at desks on each of which is a small Union Jack flag. When a member is prepared to deal – either buy or sell at a given price – their flag is lowered. When all the flags have been lowered, a price is struck and all transactions matched. The price struck is then published.

Since April 1969, the London Gold Market has been functioning without official support or intervention.

In 1977, efforts were made, particularly by the US, to have gold phased out of the international monetary system. European countries resisted this in the belief that the most effective way of achieving international monetary law and order lay in organising a new system in which gold would play a significant part. This may not have happened officially but the price of gold today is seen as an index of international opinion. The higher it goes, the less faith there is in national currencies and vice versa.

In 1982, gold contracts, previously offered in sterling, started being offered in US dollars. This was to correspond to the international bullion price which has always been quoted in dollars, and to avoid currency price fluctuation influencing the market.

Regulation

In the late 1980s, major changes took place in the regulatory environment governing the trading of securities (that is, shares and other financial instruments), with the object of increasing both competition and investor protection.

Taken in conjunction with the Companies Act, 1985 and the Companies Securities (Insider Dealing) Act, 1985, the Financial Services Act, 1986 established a system of self regulation of the securities market by those engaged in its operation. This system extended the mixture of legislation and non-statutory regulation previously in force, while having a major impact on the manner of operation of the market.

Companies Act, 1985

The Companies Act, 1985 was essentially a consolidating act, bringing together and updating legislation from a number of previous acts. Typically, when companies legislation is amended, the amendments are not incorporated back into the original legislation but exist in new legislation side-by-side with the old. Over time, this becomes unwieldy, and a consolidating act is used to pull everything together. For example, companies legislation was consolidated in 1948, 1969 and again in 1985.

One provision of particular interest to the operation of the securities market is the requirement placed on investors to disclose the holding of a three per cent or greater interest in the shares of a public company within five days of the acquisition of the holding (or of the transaction that brought the holding above three per cent).

The notification must be made to the company in which the holding is held and to The Stock Exchange; the Panel on Take-overs and Mergers may also require notification to be made to the market by noon on the day following receipt of notification by the company. The requirement for disclosure also operates if several persons are acting together (as a 'concert party'), even though none of the persons may have individually broached the three per cent threshold.

Companies Securities (Insider Dealing) Act, 1985

Insider dealing is trading in securities with knowledge not generally available to the market – typically, information secured through one's position inside the company or in connection with someone who is, hence the term – thus securing an unfair advantage over other investors. The Act forbids any person who is, or at any time in the preceding six months has been, knowingly connected with a company from dealing on a recognised exchange in the shares of that company if he has information that:

- He holds by virtue of being connected with the company
- It would be reasonable to expect a person so connected, and in the position in which he is so connected, not to disclose except for the proper performance of the functions attaching to that position
- He knows is unpublished price-sensitive information in relation to those securities.

Exceptions are made for persons who need to deal in the shares of the company for good reason. For example, some companies insist that newly appointed directors must buy a minimum number of shares in order to hold the position of director.

Conviction for insider dealing leads to imprisonment for up to two years and/or a fine.

Corporate governance

The large corporate failures and associated scandals of the late 1980s focused attention on the issue of corporate governance – the way in which companies are managed.

In May 1991, the Financial Reporting Council, the London Stock Exchange and the accountancy profession established the Committee on the Financial Aspects of Corporate Governance, chaired by Sir Adrian Cadbury – hence the 'Cadbury committee'.

The recommendations of the Cadbury Committee in its report focus on a Code of Best Practice, which dealt with a number of matters:

- The Board of Directors:
  > The Board should meet regularly
  > There should be a clear division of responsibilities at the head of a company
  > The Board should include non-executive directors of sufficient calibre and number
  > There should be schedule of matters specifically reserved for full board consideration *
  > There should be a procedure for directors in the furtherance of their duties to take independent professional advice at the company's expense *

> All directors should have access to the advice and services of the company's Secretary

- Non-executive directors:
  > An independent judgement should be brought to bear
  > The majority should be independent of management, and free from any other business or other relationships which could materially interfere with the exercise of independent judgement
  > The appointment should be for specified terms, and re-appointment should not be automatic *
  > A formal process should be used to select non-executive directors, and this should be a matter for the whole Board *
- Executive directors:
  > Service contracts should not exceed three years without shareholders' approval *
  > There should be full and clear disclosure of emoluments *
  > Pay should be subject to the recommendations of a remuneration committee made up wholly or mainly of non-executive directors *
- Reporting and controls
  > The Board has a duty to present a balanced and understandable assessment of the company's position
  > An objective and professional relationship should be maintained with the auditors
  > An audit committee should be established of at least three non-executive directors, with written terms of reference *
  > The directors should explain their responsibility for preparing the accounts next to a statement by the auditors about their reporting responsibilities *
  > The directors should report on the effectiveness of the company's system of internal control *
  > The directors should report that the company is a going concern *.

The Committee recommended that listed companies should confirm their compliance with the Code – or give reasons for non-compliance – in annual reports for years ended after 30 June 1993. The Committee also recommended that the company's auditors should review compliance with those aspects of the Code marked with an asterisk (*) above.

The Stock Exchange has made the requirement for a statement of compliance with the Code of Best Practice a continuing obligation of listing.

The Committee has recommended that its sponsors, convened by the Financial Reporting Council, should appoint a new committee by the end of June 1995 to examine how far compliance with the Code has progressed, how far its other recommendations have been implemented, and whether the Code needs updating. In the meantime, the present Committee will remain responsible for reviewing the implementation of its proposals.

In addition to the Code of Best Practice, the Committee made a number of other recommendations, dealing mainly with changes in law and regulation, as well as accounting and auditing guidance, which will be necessary to achieve the Committee's objectives. The full report of the Committee (including the Code of Best Practice) is available from Gee, South Quay Plaza, 183 Marsh Wall, London E14 9FS.

Financial Services Act, 1986

The Financial Services Act, 1986 (FSA) was introduced as part of the system of self-regulation that now acts as a control on the operation of securities markets in the UK. The concept that those involved in the markets were best able to regulate the markets led to the creation of a number of new bodies to regulate securities traders and others, while existing professional bodies (for example, those representing accountants) were recognised for the purposes of regulating their members under the FSA.

Inter alia, the Financial Services Act:

- Defined investments
- Made it a criminal offence to carry on investment business without authorisation
- Made it a criminal offence to make a false or misleading statement (a) with the intention of inducing someone to buy or sell investments, or (b) to deceive as to the true value of investments
- Established the Securities and Investments Board (SIB), which in turn created five self-regulatory organisations (SROs) and a number of recognised professional bodies (RPBs) and recognised investment exchanges (RIEs).

Under the FSA, a person is deemed to be carrying on investment business if, as a business, he:

- Buys and sells investments
- Arranges for others to buy and sell investments
- Manages investments on behalf of others
- Advises others on investments
- Operates a collective investment scheme.

Persons deemed to be carrying on investment business must obtain authorisation to do so. The authorisation will be restricted to those kinds of business that the person is competent to undertake. Authorisation may be sought for any, or all, of:

- Dealing: Buying, selling, subscribing for or underwriting investments, whether as principal or agent
- Arranging deals: Making, offering or agreeing to make arrangements whereby a third person may deal in an investment
- Managing: Where a third party's investments are managed at the discretion of the manager
- Advising
- Establishing, operating or winding up collective investment schemes.

A person is exempt from the requirement for authorisation if he:

- Is investing on his own account
- Is a trustee not specifically paid for the provision of investment management services
- Gives investment advice purely as a consequence of advice on non-investment matters.

In this last instance, a distinction is drawn between:

- 'Necessary' investment advice: Given as part of non-investment advice and inseparable from it
- 'Incidental' investment advice: Given as part of one's business but not a major part of it
- 'Mainstream' investment advice.

Carrying on investment business without authorisation is a criminal offence, punishable by fines and imprisonment. There is no need for the prosecutor to prove fraud (indeed, it may not exist), merely lack of authorisation. However, a person authorised for one aspect of investment business (say, advising) who conducts another function (say, dealing) without authorisation is not guilty of a criminal offence, though he is still liable to sanction. Contracts entered into by an unauthorised person are not enforceable by him, though they may be enforced against him.

Authorised advisers may act as either as:

- Independent advisers, providing clients with advice on the most appropriate investment from all those available on the market
- 'Tied' agents selling only the products of a single company.

The separation is known as 'polarisation' and the client must be informed at the start of any discussions whether the adviser is independent or tied – there is no halfway house.

Investments are defined as:

- Stocks and shares in UK or foreign companies and unincorporated bodies
- Debentures, loan stock, bonds and certificates of deposit
- Government and other public securities, gilt edged stocks, local authority bonds and bonds issued by foreign governments and international organisations
- Warrants entitling the holder to subscribe for shares or bonds
- Certificates conferring rights to acquire, dispose of, underwrite or convert shares, bonds or warrants
- Units in collective investment schemes (for example, unit trusts) and shares in open-ended investment companies
- Options on currency and on any other investment
- Futures contracts made for investment purposes
- Contracts for differences
- Endowment and unit-linked insurance policies (but not pure term assurance).

The Securities and Investments Board

The Securities and Investments Board (SIB), which was established under the FSA, is at the centre of the new system of self-regulation. Its main duty is to ensure that only 'fit and proper' persons are authorised to undertake investment business.

Although individuals may obtain authorisation to carry on investment business direct from SIB, authorisation is generally obtained from one of the self regulatory organisations (SROs) or recognised professional bodies (RPBs).

SIB sets the basic rules under which the markets must operate; its rulebook thus determines the scope and content of the rulebooks issued by the SROs and RPBs.

SIB rules

SIB's rules on the conduct of investment business provide that an authorised person must:

- Maintain high standards of integrity and fair dealing in conducting an investment business
- Act with due skill, care and diligence in providing any service he provides or declares himself willing to provide
- Subordinate his own interests to those of his clients and act fairly as between his clients
- Have due regard to the circumstances of his clients.

Persons authorised by SROs or RPBs will be bound by rules at least equal to these.

Each authorised person is required to comply with the rules; if the person authorised has representatives or is a limited company with employees, each representative or employee must comply with the rules. If there are more than 10 employees, procedures to ensure compliance must be recorded in writing. A review of such procedures must be carried out at least annually to ensure that they are effective.

Failure to comply with the conduct of business rules can result in the withdrawal of authorisation, effectively taking away the adviser's livelihood.

SIB's rulebooks comprise a three tier structure:

- A top tier of 'principles'
- A second tier of 'core rules' establishing the common regulatory requirements of the system
- A third tier of detailed rules, codes of conduct and guidance notes, tailored by the individual regulatory bodies to the business of their members.

Statements of Principles were issued in April 1990. These were intended to be a straightforward and universal statement of conduct expected, that:

- Clearly summarised and built on current best practice
- Would be readily understood by all those involved in financial markets
- Would be sufficiently general to apply readily to new situations, without the need for frequent amendment and updating, which was a problem with SIB's early rulebooks.

The second tier has been developed on the basis of 'adequacy' rather than 'equivalence'. Under the FSA as originally enacted, the rulebook of an SRO or RPB was required to provide investors with protection *at least equivalent* to that provided by SIB's own rulebook. The new adequacy test now looks for 'an adequate level of protection for the investor', a slightly less onerous requirement.

Some 29,000 firms and individuals have been registered under the FSA with the SROs, RPBs, or direct with SIB. Most (60 per cent) are authorised by RPBs, with only a handful being authorised by SIB direct.

A central register of authorised persons is held by SIB and may be accessed via:

- PRESTEL, BT's electronic information service
- SIB's Public Information Office (071 929 3652)
- Purchasing copies of the register on magnetic tape (these are used by service providers to provide a commercial information service to the public).

Certified copies of register entries are available from SIB's Public Information Office for £1.

Investor compensation

SIB operates an investor compensation scheme through an independent management company, Investors Compensation Scheme Limited. Its objectives are:

- To reimburse investors for losses falling within the scheme
- To do so speedily and with as little formality, and as much sympathy, as possible
- To protect the industry (which pays for the scheme) by economy in the use of resources, by carefully investigating all claims and, having paid claims, by chasing hard in each liquidation to win back as much as possible of the cash paid out.

Each investor is eligible for compensation of up to £48,000, made up of 100 per cent of the first £30,000 of eligible loss and 90 per cent of the second £20,000 of eligible loss, up to a limitation of £100 million on all claims in each financial year. Compensation costs are recovered primarily by a levy on the members of the SRO of which the defaulting firm was a member; costs above a limit are borne by a levy on members of other SROs. The top £75 million of costs is covered by insurance.

Claims paid in the year to 31 March 1992 amounted to £12.5 million, up from £1.8 million the year before. The cost of compensation for all those who invested in the 35 firms that failed in 1991-2 could reach £37 million, including management expenses.

SROs, RPBs and other regulatory bodies

The five SROs set up under the FSA were:

- The Association of Futures Brokers and Dealers (AFBD)
- The Financial Intermediaries, Managers and Brokers' Regulatory Organisation (FIMBRA)
- The Investment Management Regulatory Organisation (IMRO)
- The Life Assurance and Unit Trust Regulatory Organisation (LAUTRO)
- The Securities Association (TSA).

On 1 April 1991, the AFBD and TSA merged to form the Securities and Futures Authority (SFA).

On 1 July 1993, the Personal Investment Authority (PIA) commenced operations with the purpose of becoming an SRO though, at the time of writing, it had not been approved by SIB as an SRO. The PIA has been formed to regulate dealing in investments and managing and advising on investments for private investors, thus bringing together in one regulatory body functions which at present are covered by several – in particular, by FIMBRA and LAUTRO.

Each SRO, as their names suggest, covers a different sector of the securities market. There is, however, some slight overlap between the scope of the SROs in authorising investment activities in order to avoid the possible, though unlikely, situation of a single business having to make applications to several SROs in order to secure authorisation for all of its activities.

The SROs must have:

- A governing body whose membership is balanced between the interests of different members and between their interests and those of the public
- An effective 'scope' rule, to preclude its members carrying on investment business of a kind with which the SRO is not concerned (unless the member is otherwise authorised or exempted)
- Rules and practices such as to ensure that its members are fit and proper to carry on investment business of the kind with which the SRO is concerned. These must be at least as effective as SIB's own requirements for direct authorisation
- Fair and reasonable rules and practices relating to the admission and expulsion of members, including provision for appeals
- The ability to offer an adequate level of protection to investors
- Adequate arrangements for effective monitoring and enforcement of compliance with its rules
- Financial resources and personnel sufficient to carry out its function
- Effective arrangements for the investigation of complaints from members of the public against its members or itself.

The Investment Management Regulatory Organisation

IMRO was originally formed by members of the Accepting Houses Committee and widened to include insurance companies, clearing banks and representatives of advisors' associations.

Its members are engaged in

- Investment management, either as the sole or main activity of the firm or discretionary management services distinct from its other services
- Management and operation of collective investment schemes
- Acting as trustee of regulated collective investment schemes
- Investment management of investment trusts

- In-house pension fund management
- Acting as pension fund trustee
- Providing investment advice (other than corporate finance advice) to institutional or corporate customers
- Advising on and arranging deals in investments where this is incidental to the main investment activity of the firm.

The Financial Intermediaries, Managers and Brokers' Regulatory Organisation

FIMBRA came into being following a change of name and constitution of The National Association of Security Dealers and Investment Managers (NASDIM). It is primarily concerned with regulating the provision of services of independent investment intermediaries to retail customers (that is, to members of the public).

Its members' primary activities are:

- Advising on and arranging deals in life assurance and units in authorised unit trusts and similar collective investment schemes
- Providing investment advisory and management services to retail customers, including advising on and arranging deals in securities (including Government and other public securities, but not futures, options or contracts for differences).

The Life Assurance and Unit Trust Regulatory Organisation

LAUTRO's regulatory scope includes the regulation of the marketing activities of its members, their employees and appointed representatives, in relation to life assurance and unit trust based products, including:

- Long term insurance contracts
- Units in UK authorised unit trusts
- Units in overseas collective investment schemes (recognised by SIB)
- 'Type A' non-discretionary Personal Equity Plans (PEPs).

LAUTRO's members are insurance companies, friendly societies and managers of collective investment schemes. It has some 600 members and 180,000 representatives recorded on its register as being attached to members.

Its Board consists of 18 members, drawn:

- 7 from the life offices
- 4 from the unit trust companies
- 1 from the friendly societies
- 6 to represent the public interest.

Six committees – Executive, Membership, Selling Practices, Advertising and Product Disclosure, Commissions, and Monitoring – carry out the policies set by the Board.

In November 1989, LAUTRO began Periodic Inspection Visits (PIVs) to the offices of its members to monitor their compliance with its rules.

The Association of Futures Brokers and Dealers

The AFBD merged with The Securities Association (see below) on 1 April 1991 to form the Securities and Futures Authority.

It was originally formed by:

- The London International Financial Futures Exchange (LIFFE)
- The London Futures and Options Exchange (London FOX), which returned to its original name – London Commodity Exchange (1986) Limited – on 1 September 1993
- The International Petroleum Exchange
- The London Metal Exchange.

It was intended to be the recognised SRO for investment business in futures and options.

The Securities Association

The Securities Association (TSA), which was one of the original five SROs set up under the FSA, merged with the AFBD on 1 April 1991 to form the Securities and Futures Authority.

The Securities and Futures Authority

The Securities and Futures Authority (SFA), formed from the merger in April 1991 of the AFBD and TSA, authorises some 1,000 firms and 30,000 individuals. Its primary role is to protect the investor, both professional and private, by setting and enforcing suitable standards to which investment businesses must adhere.

Its Rule Book comprises five chapters:

- General: SFA's rules, their application, amendment and waiver
- Authorisation: The application process, the documentary requirements, the register categories, the 'fit and proper person' test, and procedures for notifying SFA of changes in a member's details
- Financial Regulation: Members' accounting records and controls, capital adequacy, financial reporting and auditing, client money and property

- Conduct of Business/Unsolicited Calls: Investor categories, the use of intermediaries, general business requirements, dealing, the keeping of records and compliance
- Enforcement and Discipline: The monitoring of members, investigation, warnings and disciplinary proceedings, settlement, protective intervention and appeals against decisions.

The Financial Regulation requirements are concerned with the relationship between a member firm's total capital requirement and its qualifying capital; at no time may the former exceed the latter.

Total capital requirement is composed of:

- Base requirement: The higher of an absolute minimum or a proportion of the firm's adjusted annual expenditure, to ensure that the firm will be able to meet its expenses on an ongoing basis
- Position risk requirement: To reflect the market risks to which a firm may be exposed as a result of holding positions in securities or other financial instruments as a principal
- Counterparty risk requirement: To reflect the risk that a firm's counterparties (that is, those it does business with) will fail to perform their contracts with the firm.

Qualifying capital is a calculated figure representing total available liquid resources net of all liabilities.

The Board of SFA comprises 27 people, representing a balance between the interests of different members and between the interest of members and the public. It is the major forum for all procedural and policy decision making and meets once a fortnight.

Recognised Professional Bodies

The concept of RPBs was established by SIB to cope with members of professional bodies, who while not being involved in investment business full-time, nonetheless had some involvement incidental to their main work. Authorisation, it was believed, would be best secured in these cases through the adviser's own professional body. Thus, under the Financial Services Act, a professional body may secure authorisation for its members through its own recognition by SIB. In order to do so, a body must have in place, or establish, rules of conduct for investment business and investor protection that provide an adequate level of protection.

The bodies recognised by SIB as RPBs are:

- The Chartered Association of Certified Accountants
- The Institute of Actuaries

- The Institute of Chartered Accountants in England & Wales
- The Institute of Chartered Accountants in Ireland
- The Institute of Chartered Accountants of Scotland
- The Insurance Brokers Registration Council
- The Law Society
- The Law Society of Northern Ireland
- The Law Society of Scotland.

The essentials for recognition of a professional body by SIB are systems for:

- Monitoring accounting records, clients' money and conduct of business
- Investigation and complaint
- Promotion and maintenance of standards
- Enforcement of its regulations by the RPB.

Members of a professional body whose main business is not investment business may obtain authorisation from their professional body; if their income from investment business exceeds the suggested threshold of 20 per cent, authorisation from an appropriate SRO must be sought.

Recognised Investment Exchanges

The final piece of the regulatory system established by the FSA was the recognition of investment exchanges (RIEs). An exchange is defined as any place or legal entity involved in drawing together people doing investment business; an RIE is one recognised by SIB under the FSA.

SIB recognises one clearing house (The London Clearing House Limited) and the following six exchanges:

- LIFFE
- OMLX – The London Securities and Derivatives Exchange Limited (an offspring of the Swedish Options Exchange that has been operating in London since 1989 and was recognised as an RIE in 1990)
- The International Petroleum Exchange
- The London Commodity Exchange
- The London Metal Exchange
- The Stock Exchange.

In addition, certain overseas exchanges (ORIEs), which SIB considers offer a reasonable level of investor protection and which have agreed to co-operate with SIB on issues arising from transactions for UK investors, are recognised as investment exchanges by the Treasury. There are now 27 ORIEs, including Globex and the Sydney Futures Exchange.

Other regulatory bodies

There is a core of non-statutory regulation within the City, which acts to protect investors. The key bodies involved in this are discussed below.

The City Panel on Take-overs and Mergers

The Panel is based in The Stock Exchange building and comprises:

- A director-general
- Two deputies
- A panel of 12 City representatives.

Their work in reviewing take-overs and mergers is based on the City Code, first published in 1968 and updated. The permanent staff of the Panel provide interpretations of the Code, but where cases are contested, the Panel itself meets. Decisions of the Panel may be appealed to an Appeals Committee.

The core rules of the Code are:

- A company may bid for up to 29.9 per cent of another company's shares without launching a full bid. Beyond this threshold, it must make an offer for all remaining shares, at the highest price paid so far
- All shareholders must be treated evenly
- Before an offer is announced, no one who has knowledge of it may deal in the shares of either the target or bidding company
- Once an offer is announced, all transactions must be reported to the Panel, The Stock Exchange, and the press (here, 'press' is usually taken to mean the key financial and national papers)
- Companies defending a bid must not do anything without shareholder approval 'which could effectively result in a *bona fide* offer being frustrated, or in the shareholders of the offeree company being denied an opportunity to decide on its merits'.

Throughout a take-over or merger, the Panel's staff are available for consultation and, with The Stock Exchange, they monitor transactions in the shares of the companies involved.

If the Code is believed to have been breached, the chairman of the offending company is invited to appear before the Panel – few refuse such an invitation. It is an informal meeting, with no rules of evidence or permanent records; nonetheless, the Panel is a legal entity and its decisions may be reviewed by the Courts.

If the Panel finds that a breach has been committed, it may:

- Censure the person/company there and then
- Issue a press release, setting out its conclusions and reasons
- Refer the case to a professional association, The Stock Exchange, the Department of Trade and Industry, or the Serious Fraud Office.

The Office of Fair Trading

The Office of Fair Trading was set up in 1973 under the Fair Trading Act. It is a non-Ministerial government department headed by a Director General of Fair Trading who appoints his own staff, generally from the ranks of established civil servants. The Secretary of State for Trade and Industry appoints the Director General of the OFT.

The Office's activities fall into three main areas:

- Consumer policy: Proposing and promoting changes in law and practice in the interests of consumers and monitoring the adoption of codes of practice
- Regulatory: Taking legal action (when possible) against undesirable trade practices and making recommendations for new legislation
- Information: The Office conducts an annual survey of consumer dissatisfaction and provides information and advice to the public. It monitors consumer complaints correspondence to the Department of the Environment, the Department of Health, and the Trading Standards (or Consumer Protection) Department, which are run by local authorities and independent of the OFT. Complaints to Citizens Advice Bureaux and Consumer Advice Centres are also monitored.

Though important discretionary decisions remain in the hands of the Secretary of State, a close working relationship exists between the DTI and the OFT – for example, senior posts in the OFT are filled by staff on loan or secondment from the DTI.

The OFT was formed to bring together some functions previously within the DTI's scope (monopolies, mergers and consumer affairs) and others from the former Registrar of Restrictive Trading Agreements. A need to develop a more independent agency for the promotion of competition and consumer protection policies, away from the political arena, also prompted the formation of the Office.

The Director General operates under the following statutes:

- The Fair Trading Act, 1973
- The Consumer Credit Act, 1974
- The Restrictive Trade Practices Act, 1976
- The Resale Prices Act, 1976
- The Estate Agents Act, 1979
- The Competition Act, 1980
- The Financial Services Act, 1986
- European Competition Law (which takes precedence over domestic law in the event of conflict)

The Office exists to maintain a balance in competition to protect the consumer. Its research and findings are sources for both policy making and restrictive action by the Secretary of State of Trade and Industry.

The Monopolies and Mergers Commission

The Monopolies and Mergers Commission (MMC) is an independent statutory body funded by the Department of Trade and Industry. All its reports are published.

The Monopolies and Restrictive Practices Commission (the forerunner of the MMC) was established under the Monopolies and Restrictive Practices (Inquiry and Control) Act, 1948. Its role was to investigate and report on monopolies and monopolistic conditions in the supply of goods and to investigate restrictive trade practices.

Under the Monopolies and Mergers Act, 1965, monopolies in the supply of services and mergers were brought within the scope of the Commission leading to the change of name. Its procedures and responsibilities have increased since then and are governed by and contained in the following Acts:

- The Fair Trading Act, 1973
- The Competition Act, 1980
- The Broadcasting Act, 1990
- Relevant privatisation statutes relating to telecommunications, gas, water, airports and electricity.

The Commission has a full-time Chairman appointed by the Secretary of State for Trade and Industry, who also appoints the members of the Commission (there is provision for up to 50 members). These represent a range of relevant experience from business, the professions, trade unions and academia.

The Commission does not have the power to initiate its own investigations. References (requests for an inquiry to be made) come from the Secretary of State for Trade and Industry, the Director General of Fair Trading or appropriate regulators in the case of privatised industries.

Once a reference has been made, the Chairman of the Commission appoints a group with a minimum of three members. Investigations are in depth, and involve both written and oral evidence. The Commission may also visit companies and has the power to require attendance of witnesses and the provision of evidence.

The Commission is primarily concerned with what is in the public interest. Section 84 of the Fair Trading Act, 1973 defines this in five points:

- Maintaining and promoting competition in the United Kingdom
- Promoting the interests of consumers

- Promoting, through competition, the development of new products and the reduction of costs
- Maintaining and promoting the balanced distribution of industry and employment
- Maintaining and promoting competitive activity in overseas markets by companies in the United Kingdom

Merger references take about three months; monopoly inquiries average between nine and fifteen months.

On completion of an inquiry, the Commission submits its report to the Secretary of State for consideration or, in certain cases, to relevant regulatory bodies. The Secretary of State's decision is usually announced at the same time as the report is published. If the Secretary finds 'against the public interest', undertakings may be made to remedy the situation. It is then the responsibility of the Director General of Fair Trading to ensure that the undertakings required are implemented.

The Serious Fraud Office

The Serious Fraud Office began operations in April 1988, following its establishment under the Criminal Justice Act, 1987. It is responsible for the investigation and prosecution of serious or complex fraud.

The SFO's immediate objectives are:

- To develop a coherent approach to the investigation of serious fraud
- To concentrate resources on the essential issues involved in complex fraud
- To speed up investigations and, where possible, the institution of criminal proceedings
- To develop expertise in specialist areas, such as Stock Exchange fraud, computer fraud and insurance fraud
- To make efficient use of new trial procedures for complex fraud cases
- To present evidence in such cases in new, clearer ways so that the average member of a jury can understand it
- To increase the proportion of successful prosecutions.

In the longer term, the SFO hopes to increase the efficiency of the criminal justice system by bringing to justice more of those involved in serious fraud, thus deterring others and maintaining confidence in the City and other financial centres.

The SFO is headed by a Director, Deputy Director and Chief Accountant, who are supported by some 100 staff. Extensive use is made of interdisciplinary teams of lawyers, accountants and other professionals with appropriate specialist expertise. These teams work closely with the police, SIB, the Bank of England, Lloyd's, the

Department of Trade and Industry, HM Customs and Excise and the Inland Revenue.

Through the Director, the SFO is accountable to the Attorney General and Parliament.

The SFO, in order to avoid duplication of effort with other investigative bodies, only handles cases in which:

- The facts and/or the law are very complex
- The sums of money at risk are substantial (that is, in excess of £5 million)
- There is great public interest or concern.

The constitutional position of the police, their accountability and their command and control structure remain unchanged by the establishment of the SFO. The responsibility for investigating serious or complex fraud is shared by the Director of the SFO and the police, but their respective powers are designed to complement each other rather than to overlap.

The Director of the SFO has extensive investigative powers, which may be delegated to others inside or outside the SFO. He may serve a written notice on a person under investigation, or a person believed to have relevant information, requiring them to answer questions and/or produce documents. It is a criminal offence (punishable by imprisonment for up to seven years or a fine or both):

- To fail to comply with an SFO requirement
- To give false or misleading statements
- To destroy or conceal relevant material.

Investment

The Financial Services Act, 1986 defines investments as:

- Stocks and shares in UK or foreign companies or unincorporated bodies
- Debentures, loan stock, bonds and certificates of deposit
- Government and public securities, local authority bonds and bonds issued by foreign governments and international organisations
- Warrants entitling the holder to subscribe for shares or bonds
- Certificates conferring rights to acquire, dispose of, underwrite or convert shares, bonds or warrants
- Units in collective investment schemes and shares in open-ended investment companies
- Options on currency and on any other investment
- Futures contracts made for investment purposes
- Contracts for differences
- Insurance policies that are investments (but not pure term insurance).

In making a choice of investment, the would-be investor should balance:

- The relative importance to him of income and capital gain
- The degree of security or risk offered
- The expected rate of return
- The tax advantages attaching to the investment
- The convenience and cost of dealing in the investment
- The ability to realise the investment.

Equity investments

Equity investments commit the holder to the entire amount of his investment without guarantee of reward, in return for a share (usually, though not always, proportionate to his investment) in such profits as may arise. Should the investment fail, the investor stands to lose the amount invested plus any further amounts guaranteed or pledged by him. In the event of failure, any refund of his investment will only come after all other claims have been met.

Loan investments, on the other hand, typically receive a fixed rate of return and, in the event of failure of the investment, may have a prior claim on whatever assets may be available for distribution.

Stocks and shares in limited companies are the primary form of equity investment. As explained in the chapter on *Company law*, the amount and types of shares are subject to the company's Articles of Association, and different classes of shares may be issued, with different rights attaching to each class.

Ordinary shares (common stock, in US parlance) are the shares found in the average company. Typically, they are issued in units with nominal values of 5p, 25p or £1.

Shares with different rights and privileges are used to weight voting rights: ordinary shares may have only 1 vote per share, while 'A' shares or 'Founders' shares' may have 10. For example, it is the difference in voting rights between classes of shares that prevents the Forte Group from exercising its numerical majority shareholding in the Savoy Hotel Group to take control.

Preferred, or preference, shares differ from ordinary shares, in two vital respects:

- They earn a fixed rate of return payable before any dividend is payable to the ordinary shareholders and thus have preference over the ordinary shares in the matter of dividends
- They have a prior claim over ordinary shareholders to repayment of capital by way of distribution of assets in the event of the winding up of the company.

Participating preference shares may attract some proportion of the profits of the company by way of dividend in excess of their fixed return, subject to the ordinary shareholders having received an agreed level of dividend. Thus, preference shares combine the security of return offered by loan investments with the possibility of 'super' returns offered by equity investments.

Convertible shares are those which may be converted, under specified conditions, into shares of a different class. An example of their use is in a management buyout where one investor may receive shares that are convertible at some future date into ordinary shares. In this way, the investor may be protected initially from the downside risk of equity investment while being offered the opportunity to share in the upside potential. Usually convertible shares are not issued on their own but are combined with preference shares to create convertible preference shares – preference shares convertible into ordinary shares.

The Companies Acts place severe restrictions on the redemption of shares by companies. This is because share capital acts as a buffer protecting creditors; reductions in share capital reduce this buffer. However, provided a company's Articles of Association permit, redeemable shares may be issued. Usually, these are combined with other attributes – to create redeemable preference shares, for example.

Classification of shares

Shares quoted on The Stock Exchange are divided into three classifications, known as:

- Alpha
- Beta
- Gamma.

New classifications for these categories were issued in early 1991, based on the 'Normal Market Size' (NMS) – the number of shares traded in a typical deal. Alpha stocks are those with an NMS of 2,000 or more and are traded by at least two market-makers on the Stock Exchange Automated Quotation system (SEAQ). All other shares are classified as beta shares. Gamma refers to preference shares, debentures, warrants and other non-equity traded instruments.

Issue of shares

The term 'subscribe for shares' comes from the fact that, when a company is formed, those who will be its first shareholders 'subscribe' their names to the Memorandum and Articles of Association, the company's constitution (that is, write their names at the foot of the Memorandum and Articles).

When the company is formed, the directors meet and allot shares, issue certificates in respect of these shares and seal them with the company's seal.

The same procedures apply on further issues of share capital: applications are received, the directors allot shares, issue certificates and so on.

Most shares are paid for in full on issue. However, a company may decide not to require full payment at the time of issue, in which case the shares are described as 'partly paid'. Many of the privatisation stocks were issued in this way. The balance of the share price is due on the terms agreed, which may be at fixed dates or on demand. Whichever it is, when money is due, the company issues a 'call' and shareholders must then meet their obligations to put up the balance of the share capital or that portion now called. Failure to do so may result in the forfeiture of the shares.

An individual shareholder's liability to the company (that is, the amount that he may be called upon to contribute to the company in the event of its liquidation) is limited to the amount of share capital paid up and the unpaid share capital not yet called.

Bonus and rights issues

Bonus, or 'scrip', shares are issued by a company free of charge to its existing shareholders in proportion to their holdings, usually as a means of distributing retained profits that cannot be paid out as dividends, either because they are not legally distributable or because of lack of cash.

In a 'rights' issue, shareholders are offered the right to buy new shares in the company in proportion to their existing holding, usually at a discount to market price. In this way, relative holdings as between shareholders can be maintained.

New issues

Shares coming to the market for the first time are called 'new issues'. If the company itself is new to the market, the term 'flotation' is used.

New issues come in three main forms:

- Offers for sale
- Placings
- Introductions.

Offers for sale may be made either as fixed price offers or as tenders. Fixed price offers involve a price being quoted by the company; would-be shareholders who wish to buy at this price apply for shares. The process of allotment then takes place. In a tender situation, would-be shareholders offer to buy a number of shares at a price they themselves set. The company assesses all such offers and then 'strikes' a price so as to sell all the shares and raise the funds needed. If individuals have offered the strike price or higher, they will receive shares, with any excess offered over the strike price being refunded (this assumes that the tender amount must be included with the tender application, which is usually the case). Those who offered less than the strike price receive no shares and are refunded their money.

Offers for sale, whether by fixed price or by tender, are preceded by a prospectus, which explains the background to the company and the share issue and is the formal 'offer' document. Because a prospectus invites members of the public to invest their money in the company, great care is paid to its content. The detailed rules for prospectuses are laid down by The Stock Exchange.

Placings are more discreet than offers for sale, which often attract a great deal of razzmatazz. In a placing, the sponsoring merchant bank will 'place' the bulk of the shares with their clients and offer the rest to other institutions. The price will be set so as to ensure that all the shares are taken up. The effective discount that results is intended to ensure a good market in the company's shares when trading begins. In this way, the company avoids the cost of an offer for sale, though it may not receive as much fresh capital as under the tender method.

Introductions usually occur when a share, already listed on another exchange, is 'introduced' to the market. A limited number of new shares may change hands.

Buying and selling shares

No dealing in shares now takes place on the floor of The Stock Exchange. Most dealing takes place on computer, between market makers and brokers using SEAQ terminals.

When an investor asks a broker to buy or sell shares for him, he may specify a price (meaning that he does not want to pay more than this and, if the broker cannot buy or sell – whichever he has been asked to do – within this limit, the broker must not deal) or ask the broker to buy or sell 'at best', the best price available. If the broker is also a market maker, he must look outside his firm to other market makers to obtain the best price for his client. Brokers now record the times at which shares were bought or sold so as to be able to prove that they dealt at the best price then available.

The flow of events in a typical dealing transaction (or 'bargain') is:

- The client gives his instructions
- The executive who takes the order instructs the in-house dealer
- The dealer checks both with the in-house market maker and external market makers
- The best price is identified
- The deal is agreed and reported to The Stock Exchange by both parties
- The executive informs the contracts departments who prepare a contract note, summarising the transaction and billing the client
- The contract note, which confirms to the client that his instructions have been properly carried out, is sent to the client
- The client pays on or before the settlement date
- Some weeks later, the shares are transferred and a certificate is issued by the company in the name of the client, the new holder.

For this service, the client pays a commission to the broker.

When the two parties to a deal report the transaction to The Stock Exchange, they report the following information to the Central Checking section:

- Security title and class
- Quantity and whether bought or sold
- Price
- Other party to the transaction
- Time of dealing

- Settlement due date
- Whether dealt as principal or agent
- Any special conditions attaching to the transaction
- Client reference number.

Once this information has been checked, it is confirmed to both parties and a binding contract then exists. All transactions go through The Stock Exchange's computer system, TALISMAN (Transfer Accounting, Lodgement for Investors, Stock MANagement for principals) and pass through nominee accounts in the name of SEPON (Stock Exchange POol Nominees).

Stock market indices

Share price performance is critical to good investment returns. Over the years a number of indices have been constructed to monitor market performance. These include:

- Financial Times Ordinary Share Index (FT 30)
- Financial Times - Actuaries All-Share Index (FT-A)
- Financial Times - Stock Exchange (FT-SE 100 – known colloquially as 'Footsie')
- Financial Times - Stock Exchange Mid 250 (FT-SE Mid 250)
- Financial Times - Stock Exchange Actuaries 350 (FT-SE A 350)
- Financial Times - Stock Exchange Eurotrack 100
- Financial Times - Stock Exchange Eurotrack 200
- Financial Times - Actuaries World Indices
- Morgan Stanley Capital International Indices.

Equivalent international indices include the Dow Jones (USA) and Nikkei (Japan). *A Guide to Financial Times statistics* (ISBN 1 85334 028 6) is recommended as further reading in this area.

FT 30

This index, based on the share prices of 30 leading companies, was first calculated in 1935. However, its mathematical structure means that it is not a good indicator of long term performance and other indices (see below) were developed. Nonetheless, the FT 30 is an important index, because it is easy and quick to calculate, sensitive, and widely understood.

FT-A

The FT-A Index is based on the market capitalisation of 687 companies, representing 93 per cent of total UK market capitalisation. It is a weighted arithmetic index, which means that a constituent company's share price is weighted by the number of shares it has in issue – thus a 5 per cent price change in the smallest company included in the index has less effect than the same price change in the largest company.

Its objective is to provide a long term measure of market performance. It has been calculated since 1962.

FT-SE 100

The FT-SE 100 Index, first introduced on 3 January 1984, is constructed from the share prices of the UK's top 100 companies, based on weighted market capitalisation. It is updated minute by minute, between 8.30 am and 4.30 pm, as transactions in these shares occur.

The 100 companies that make up the index account for two-thirds of total UK equity market capitalisation. The composition of the index is regularly reviewed. Companies ranking 90th or higher by market capitalisation are considered for inclusion and those at or below the 110th position are considered for exclusion; companies between 90th and 110th positions are on a short list for inclusion or exclusion as vacancies arise. Changes to the index are implemented on the first business days of January, April, July, and October.

Companies automatically excluded from the index are those:

- Incorporated and/or registered for tax purposes outside the UK and, therefore, resident overseas
- Subsidiaries of a company already included in the index
- Subject to large concentrated holdings (75 per cent or more of the issued capital) that effectively limit their liquidity.

A large new issue, amounting to 1.5 per cent or more of the FT-SE capitalisation, would be considered for inclusion at the earliest possible opportunity.

The objectives in constructing the index were to provide:

- A real time indicator of market trends
- A real time index to support options and futures trading.

FT-SE Mid 250 and FT-SE A 350

The FT-SE Mid 250 comprises the 250 shares immediately below those included in the FT-SE 100; the FT-SE A 350 is a combination of the FT-SE 100 and FT-SE Mid 250. Both were set up in 1992, though they have been calculated back to 31 December 1985.

FT-SE Eurotrack 100

This index, launched in December 1990, provides:

- A real time measure of market performance of Continental Europe's securities markets, comparable to the UK FT-SE 100
- Close tracking and correlation with the Financial Times - Actuaries World Index and the Morgan Stanley Capital International Index

- Calculations in Deutsche Marks, with price movements of constituent stocks in local currency.

It is based on the weighted market capitalisations of Europe's top 100 companies. The rules for inclusion in, and exclusion from, the index of companies are similar to the those for the FT-SE 100.

FT-SE Eurotrack 200
This index, launched on 25 February 1991, effectively combines the FT-SE 100 (UK equities) and FT-SE Eurotrack 100 (non-UK European equities) in a pan-European index. All stocks included in the index are traded on a single market under a common set of dealing rules. The index is calculated every minute and published in Ecu.

FT-Actuaries World indices
These are complied jointly by the *Financial Times*, Goldman Sachs, and County NatWest Securities in conjunction with the Institute of Actuaries and the Faculty of Actuaries and provide:
- Performance analysis for each country/region, in sterling, US dollars and local currency for 'This Week', 'This Month', 'This Quarter' and 'Year to Date'
- Performance highlights of world markets for the current month
- Constituent history, showing additions/deletions of stock during the current quarter.

Morgan Stanley Capital International indices
Provided by the investment bank Morgan Stanley, these indices include regional indices, country indices and international industry group performances, summarising stock market developments world-wide.

Other investments

The FSA lists many other types of investments, some of which are covered below.

Debentures

Debentures are a loan to a company, evidenced by certificates and secured on some or all of the assets of the company. A debenture differs from a bank loan in that it is made under a deed and is a negotiable instrument. Debentures are usually redeemable and are sometimes convertible into the company's equity.

The charge on company assets is usually a floating charge (that is, over all the assets of the company) in order to allow the management flexibility in trading. On default of the terms of the debenture (by, for example, non-payment of interest on the due date), the floating charge crystallises into a fixed charge on the specific assets covered and held by the company at the time of default. A trustee is appointed to supervise the company's obligations under the debenture deed.

Loan stock

Loan stock is usually unsecured, ranking with other unsecured creditors in the event of a company liquidation. Variants include loan stock convertible into equity, stock subordinated to other creditors or guaranteed by other group companies.

Certificates of deposit

Certificates of deposit (CDs) are received in exchange for cash placed on deposit with a bank and, being bearer documents (that is, the owner's name is not written on them and thus the holder is presumed to be the owner) are negotiable instruments, tradable on the London discount market.

The price achieved on a CD will reflect the rate of interest being earned by the deposit as well as the time left to run before maturity.

Government securities

It is easy to forget that the government has no money of its own, merely what it can raise by way of taxes. Often this is insufficient to meet the many calls on the public purse and resort must be had to borrowing, both at central and local government level.

Government securities are considered to be 'safe as houses' and the rate of interest (the 'coupon') attaching to them reflects the fact that no British government has ever defaulted on a loan or failed to meet its obligations on its borrowing. The tag, 'gilt edged stock', is often used in a way that suggests that it indicates the regard in which they are held; in fact, the name arises because the early certificates for government securities were issued with gold edges.

Local authority stocks and bonds

Local authorities also raise funds through public borrowings; in such cases, they issue stocks or bonds for public subscription. The usual period of issue of local authority stocks and bonds is six years although some are undated (that is, they have no fixed maturity or redemption date). 'Yearling' bonds are those with a one year life.

Like government securities, the rate of interest offered reflects the inherent security though, because they are regarded as less 'glamorous' than other investments, local authorities will often offer a premium to attract investors.

Most public issues are for specific purposes, for specific periods of time, at competitive rates of interest and are redeemable at a known future date. Interest may be payable:

- In the normal way on the nominal value of the stock or bond
- Partly through a premium on redemption, with a lower rate of interest during the life of the stock or bond
- Partly through 'deep discounting' the offer price (that is, offering £100 nominal value of stock for, say, £65).

Government securities (gilts) are a poor investment when interest rates are rising and a good investment when interest rates are falling. This is because their market price is established by reference to the yield (the rate of return on the market price, not the nominal value) which must be competitive. A gilt offering 4 per cent interest on £100 nominal value is poor value when interest rates are at 8 per cent; such a stock might be expected to trade at £50 per £100 of nominal value, at which point the yield (4 per cent earned on an investment of £50) equates to market rates of interest. If interest rates fall to 6 per cent, the market price would rise to the point where the yield equated to market rates – in this case, the price would rise to £67.

Gilts are classified as:

- Short-dated: Less than five years to run to redemption
- Medium-dated: Between five and 15 years to run
- Long-dated: More than 15 years to run
- Undated or irredeemable: Those with no final date specified for redemption.

Warrants

There are occasions when it may not be appropriate for a company to issue shares or debentures but, nonetheless, it may need to raise funds. In such situations, a company may issue warrants, a negotiable instrument entitling the holder to subscribe for shares in the company at some future time.

Warrants typically specify:

- The terms under which they may be exercised
- The period in which they may, or the date by which they must, be exercised

- The price at which they can be exercised, often set at a discount to the likely price at the time of exercise
- The circumstances under which they become exercisable.

The value of a warrant depends on the discount from the current market price of the shares represented by the exercise price. The greater the discount, the greater the value of the warrant.

Rights

A company may issue shareholders or other persons with the right to buy shares at a specific price in certain circumstances. Warrants are a form of rights.

However, in order not to dilute the relative shareholdings of existing shareholders, a company may offer existing shareholders the 'right' to subscribe for new shares in proportion to their existing holdings, usually at a discount to the current market price. If all shareholders take up their rights, the company will raise the money it needs without broadening its shareholder base, and existing shareholders will have preserved their relative shareholdings.

Individual shareholders may not wish to take up their rights, despite the discount from market price. They are free to sell their rights in the market (depending on the terms of the rights issues – a recent development has been rights issues where shareholders who do not take up their rights may not sell them on). The greater the discount from market price that the rights price represents, the greater the value of the rights.

The FSA mentions the right to buy or sell shares, bonds or warrants or dispose of, underwrite or convert them.

The right to buy shares, particularly where it is exercisable at a price below the current market price, is obviously valuable. But what benefit does the right to sell shares confer? Put simply, it guarantees a sale price. So long as the market price is above the exercise price, the right to sell has no value; but if prices fall suddenly below the exercise price, then the right to sell at a price now higher than market takes on a value based on the difference.

Underwriting is the process whereby an institution agrees, for a fee, to buy any of the shares of a company not sold in a flotation. Depending on the institution's view of a company's long term prospects, the right to underwrite shares may or may not be valuable.

The right to convert to equity may be built in at the time of issue, as in convertible preference shares. Alternatively, it may exist separately from shares. In this way, the holder of preference shares might buy the right to convert into equity.

Collective investment schemes

Investors are often unwilling to commit large sums to individual investments; they prefer to spread the risk by investing in a number of securities. However, diversification of risk is not easily obtained since it requires large sums for investment, as well as time and expertise to manage the resulting portfolio.

Collective investment schemes solve this problem. Individual investors entrust their funds to a manager who invests on their behalf. Each investor has a share in the investment pool proportionate to their investment. The larger sums available for investment, as well as the professional expertise of the manager, allow the construction of a portfolio with adequately dispersed risk. These investments are best suited to long term investment.

There are two kinds of collective investment schemes:

- Closed end schemes
- Open end schemes.

Closed end schemes set out to raise a certain amount of money for investment. Once this has been raised, no further funds are sought. The money is invested and investors receive ongoing dividends as well as capital growth. When the fund is liquidated, they receive a share of the liquidation proceeds proportionate to their original investment. If, before the liquidation of the fund, investors wish to realise their investment, they can trade their investment on the market. Investment trusts and many of the BES funds are examples of closed end schemes.

Open end schemes have no limit on the amount of funds that they seek to raise. Investors are free to add to the fund at any time and also free to realise their investment by selling their holding back to the manager. For this reason, unit trusts, which are a form of open end scheme, tend to keep a proportion of their fund in cash, ready to meet investors' needs to realise capital.

The main differences between investment trusts (closed end) and unit trusts (open end) are:

- Share prices for investment trusts (which, strictly, are companies and not trusts) usually stand at a discount (averaging 20 per cent) to the market value of the shares held. This is because market perception is that these holdings are so large that they could only be disposed of at a discount to market price; this discount is thus built into the valuation of the trust
- Investment trusts may borrow; unit trusts may not
- Unit trusts must redeem shares from investors; investment trusts are not so bound
- Because investment trusts are closed end, fund managers do not have to allow for early redemption by investors nor find

suitable investments for freshly introduced funds, and are thus able to look for long term opportunities in the market
- Investment trusts must distribute a minimum of 85 per cent of their income but may not distribute capital gains
- Investment trusts may invest up to 15 per cent of their assets in a single security; unit trusts are limited to five per cent
- Unit trusts must invest in quoted securities only; investment trusts may invest in unquoted securities as well as property, treasury bills and bank deposits
- Investment trusts may only advertise when they are launched (that is, while they are seeking funds); unit trust may advertise at any time (since they are always open to fresh funds).

Going against the logic of collective investment, which is to spread the risk by investing a number of small sums together across a diversified portfolio, many collective schemes specialise in particular industry sectors, countries or type of shares.

Options

Options, like rights, take their value from the difference between their exercise price and the market price of the underlying security.

Options to buy shares are 'call' options; options to sell are 'put' options.

To understand how options work, read the section on Options in the chapter on *Treasury*.

Corporate finance

The principal areas of corporate finance covered in this chapter are:

- Raising finance
- Mergers, acquisitions and disposals.

This chapter also covers management buy-outs, as a specific form of raising finance, though it does not seek to address the world of take-over bids.

Raising finance

When a company seeks to raise finance, it must first determine the mix of debt and equity for the business, recognising that while debt may be the cheapest form of finance, it is also the least flexible since it will impose a fixed interest and debt repayment burden on the company. If a company allows itself to become too highly geared (that is, it has over borrowed), it could experience serious financial difficulties if its business is disrupted for any reason. The risk of failure is heightened because a significant proportion of operating cash flow will be earmarked for interest and debt repayments leaving little margin for error. Conversely, a company with a very low gearing level may not be gaining any benefits from the effect of leverage.

Methods of raising equity finance

The largest source of equity finance is the stock market. New issues have been described in the previous chapter. Other sources are the venture capital market and corporate venturing.

Venture capital

Venture capital is a source of medium/long term equity finance where the investor obtains a return from an income stream as well as from the growth in the value of the investment over time. The funds will generally be provided in the form of ordinary and/or preference shares. While the ordinary shares are not subject to repayment, the preference shares will normally be redeemable after eight or more years. The redemption schedule for preference shares is typically arranged in the expectation that the venture capitalists would achieve an exit for their investment prior to the redemption date, either by way of trade sale or flotation.

Corporate venturing
Corporate venturing takes place when a large corporation invests in a small company. The large corporation provides the additional financial resources necessary and is able to become involved in new areas of expertise. The smaller company gains access to cash resources, wider management skills and technical expertise.

Methods of raising debt finance

The following are the main types of debt finance available to companies seeking to borrow funds:

• **Short term debt finance**	Bank overdrafts Debt factoring and invoice discounting
• **Medium term debt finance**	Term loans Leasing Hire purchase Mezzanine debt Loan stock
• **Long term debt finance**	Term loans Mortgage loans Loan stock

Bank overdrafts
An overdraft facility allows the borrower access to cash resources at short notice. However, banks will sometimes charge a higher interest rate on these types of facilities, as compared to normal bank loans, representing the 'price' of accessibility.

An overdraft is a very useful method for financing working capital fluctuations. The main advantage to borrowers is that these facilities can be arranged very quickly. However, they are repayable on demand, although this power is rarely exercised by banks.

Debt factoring
Debt factoring entails the purchase of a company's trade debtors by a factoring institution. Typically, the factoring company advances up to 80 per cent of the value of the trade debt at the outset and the balance, less any charges, is paid when all the debts have been collected. There are a number of variants of debt factoring under which the factor may take on all of the bad debt risk, provide credit insurance or carry out the

administration of the sales ledger and debt collection. The fee structure will obviously vary according to the level of risk assumed by the factor.

Invoice discounting is a similar service to factoring but the company retains full responsibility for collecting and administering the debts. As such, customers would not be aware that their invoices had been discounted. The company sells invoices to the factor at a discount and receives a proportion of the face value of the invoices in advance.

Bank term loan

A term loan is a loan with a predetermined repayment schedule. It is often secured on the assets of the business. The bank agrees to provide the loan at a specific time and expects to receive payment of interest and repayment of the loan in accordance with the predetermined repayment schedule.

The terms and conditions of the loan will include details of the repayment schedule and interest rate and any specific financial or commercial covenants. A financial covenant that is commonly required by banks is for the company to maintain pre-tax operating cash flows and earnings above a specified multiple of interest for the period. The multiple that banks require is typically two to four times, and will vary depending on the type of business and the general economic climate.

Leasing

Leasing allows the borrower to plan financial arrangements and may provide taxation advantages compared to the outright purchase of an asset. Although lease arrangements can vary significantly, they can be distinguished in accounting terms as:

- Finance leases
- Operating leases.

Under a finance lease, the leasing company purchases the plant or equipment and leases it to the business at an agreed rental. The business operates the equipment and, for the expected life of the equipment, takes responsibility for repairs, maintenance and insurance. The lessor therefore carries substantially all of the risks and rewards of ownership and thus, for accounting purposes, the asset would be capitalised. It is shown on the balance sheet at its 'fair value' and the financing is shown as a creditor. The monthly (or quarterly) payments under the lease are split into a capital element, which is deducted from the finance creditor, and an interest element, which is charged in the profit and loss account.

Under an operating lease, the equipment is often leased to a number of different users over its life. The leasing agreement will specify the minimum lease period and who is to have responsibility for maintenance and servicing. In accounting terms, operating lease payments are charged direct to the profit and loss account as an expense.

Hire purchase

Hire purchase (HP) is a convenient form of short term and medium term credit, related to the financing of plant and equipment. Unlike leasing, under HP agreements the equipment belongs to the business at the end of the payment period. HP agreements have relatively flexible repayment terms, are easy to arrange and may have tax benefits compared to leasing.

Mezzanine debt

Mezzanine finance is a hybrid, since it carries the characteristics of both equity and debt. Typically, it is issued as sub-ordinated debt – that is, repayment of the debt can only be made after all other secured creditors have been repaid. Mezzanine debt will also generally carry a second charge over the assets of a business, ranking behind the normal bank debt.

Due to the higher investment risk faced by mezzanine holders, as compared to pure bank lending, the mezzanine interest rate will typically be between two and four per cent above the bank interest rate. Mezzanine providers will also often require share warrants that will confer upon them the right to purchase ordinary shares at par value. These warrants, sometimes referred to as an 'equity kicker', increase the mezzanine provider's overall rate of return to between 20 and 25 per cent per annum.

Mezzanine finance can also be structured in the form of preference share capital in order to reduce apparent gearing on the balance sheet.

Loan stock

A company can raise debt finance by issuing loan stock through the financial markets. The form of the loan stock can vary significantly:

- It could have a varying period to maturity or even be a perpetual instrument
- It could have either a fixed or a floating interest rate
- It could be convertible into ordinary shares.

Unsecured loan stock can be issued by companies, usually those quoted on The Stock Exchange, and generally carries a fixed interest rate. Eurobonds are a form of loan stock that is traded.

Convertible loan stock provides investors with the option to convert all or part of the loan into a fixed number of shares in the company over a period of years. Stock that is not converted will usually become repayable on a particular date. The advantage for the company is that investors will be willing to accept a lower rate of interest on the stock because of the potential value of the conversion rights.

However, in the event that the company's share price falls below the conversion price for the loan stock, then the company is likely to be faced with the need to fund the redemption of the loan stock – a possibility for which it may not have adequately prepared. This set of circumstances has placed a number of UK companies in financial difficulties.

Mergers and acquisitions (M&A)

A merger is the integration of two similar sized businesses, where the shareholders of each business exchange their shares for shares in the new merged business. In contrast, an acquisition usually involves the integration of businesses of different sizes, where the company making the acquisition dominates the enlarged business. Acquisitions of quoted companies are colloquially known as 'take-overs'. The mechanics required to implement mergers are often the same as the methods used for acquisitions, consequently references in this section to acquisitions also include mergers.

The acquisition process

The following is the sequence of events for the acquisition of a private company:

- Decision to acquire
- Develop acquisition strategy
- Prepare detailed target criteria
- Target identification
- Plan approach & negotiation strategy
- Detailed negotiations leading to heads of agreement
- Due diligence
- Negotiate sale & purchase agreement
- Integrate acquired operations with existing businesses
- Achieve corporate objectives
- Decision to acquire (re-start sequence).

The general sequence of events for the acquisition of a quoted company is similar but, in addition, there is the requirement to follow the rules set out in the City Code on Take-overs and mergers. However, the purchaser of a publicly quoted company is unlikely to be able to obtain as much information in its due diligence stage as it would if it were purchasing a private company. In addition, the acquisition of a quoted company will be executed by way of a general offer and not a sale and purchase contract.

Decision to acquire
A well-managed company will make the decision to acquire a business following a detailed review of its own strategic objectives. Those strategic objectives may include business growth, which can be achieved by developing the existing business through organic growth or through growth by acquisition.

Develop acquisition strategy and detailed target criteria
The general acquisition criteria should be defined in the following terms:
- Strategic issues
- Commercial issues
- Financial issues
- Internal issues (management resources, timing etc.)

From these general acquisition criteria, detailed target criteria can be drawn up and targets sought.

Target identification
The company seeking an acquisition target can adopt either a 'passive' or an 'active' approach in identifying that target.

A purchaser wishing to adopt a passive approach to seeking an appropriate target will register its acquisition criteria with intermediaries and other M&A brokers. The intermediaries and brokers will then introduce potential targets to the purchaser as and when they become aware of such opportunities. In addition, the purchaser will review any other sources, including the business press and trade publications, to identify potential targets known to be for sale.

The passive purchaser can access opportunities from a number of sources:
- Intermediaries (banks, lawyers, accountants)
- M&A broking boutiques
- Trade sources
- Press.

The cost of a passive acquisition search is low; generally, intermediaries and brokers will only charge a fee for introducing a potential target if that introduction leads to a completed transaction.

An active approach to target identification involves a review of any available information to identify potential targets that satisfy the purchaser's acquisition criteria, including companies that are not known to be for sale.

The result of an acquisition search process should be a list of potential targets. It must be accepted at this stage that the purchaser will not have all the information about the potential target that he would like. Where a public company has been targeted, a hostile bid is possible, but the risks of a costly failure are clearly heightened. However, in private company deals, acquisition is only possible with co-operation of the owners, who also may be the management. Therefore, in order to obtain more information and to determine whether an offer for the company would be entertained by the current owners, an approach will be made, probably after further basic research has been undertaken. Even if the initial approach is rebuffed, it is likely that the potential bidder may consider a hostile bid or the owners reconsider their position sometime after the initial approach.

Plan approach and negotiation strategy

The method of approach will vary with the circumstances of an individual opportunity. The purchaser may be able to make an approach through an existing contact in the target company. The initial approach should be made at a sufficiently senior level to establish credibility, usually this means either the chairman or the managing director. There may be circumstances where an approach directly to the shareholders is appropriate, however careful consideration needs to be given to the implications of such a move for both the success of the bid and the continuing relationship with target's management.

Depending upon the purchaser's willingness to make open his intentions, professional advisers may be asked to make the initial approach on behalf of an unnamed interested client.

An approach is usually not made until the target has been thoroughly researched. In assessing the timing of an approach, consideration should also be given to the availability of both purchaser's and target's management – for example, the target's management is unlikely to welcome a take-over in the run up to its busy season.

Detailed negotiations to heads of agreement

When it has been established that target's owners are willing to sell, the purchaser and target will then discuss and agree outline terms for the acquisition of target. These outline terms are frequently set out formally in a document known as 'heads of agreement'. This is often the first time in the acquisition process that lawyers are involved. The heads of agreement are usually drafted in a manner such that they are not legally binding and that they merely provide an outline of each party's intentions.

Due diligence

This stage involves a detailed review of target's operations by the purchaser. This review is either performed by the acquiring company's own staff or by an independent firm of accountants (generally, the acquiring company's auditors). The results of the review are then used by the purchaser to revise his assessment of the target and provide further information for the detailed negotiations.

Negotiate sale and purchase agreement

This stage of the acquisition process requires significant input from the legal advisers of the target company and of the purchaser. Each clause in the sale and purchase agreement will be reviewed in detail and each side will negotiate variations to those clauses.

Sale and purchase agreements invariably include warranties and indemnities. These are clauses that are included to protect the purchaser and ensure that the assets and business performance he believes he is buying are genuine. A warranty allows the purchaser to seek damages to the extent that the breached warranty would have led to the purchaser paying a lower price for the target. Under a breach of indemnity, the purchaser is able to seek damages in direct proportion to the extent of the loss arising from the breach. Consequently, the vendors of companies will seek to minimise the warranties and indemnities included in the sale and purchase agreement.

The negotiation of details in the sale and purchase agreement can be particularly delicate when the target's vendors will also be target's management after the sale.

Integrate acquired operations

Once the acquisition has been completed, the purchaser will need to integrate the new acquisition into his existing business. This will include rationalisation of the acquired business to eliminate costs attributable to activities already carried out in the existing business and reorganising the combined business to maximise efficiency. The integration process will often include introduction of the purchaser's management and financial reporting systems and may include new banking arrangements. Following integration of the acquired business, the purchaser should review the business objectives and consider whether those objectives have been achieved through the acquisition.

At point, the purchaser can begin the process all over again, by seeking to identify a suitable acquisition target.

Valuation of the acquisition target

The valuation of businesses is a highly subjective process. Generally, the value of a business at a point in time derives from the future benefit that it is anticipated will result from ownership of the business. Since the value of a business relates to rewards of ownership to be derived and determined in the future, such value will be influenced by both subjective and objective considerations. It will also be influenced by the particular circumstances of the potential purchaser and vendor in a proposed transaction.

There are a number of factors that will influence the value of a company to a potential purchaser. These include:

- General industrial and economic environment
- Target's market share and position
- Target's rate of growth
- Quality and maintainability of earnings
- Quality of management
- Target's technological and production capabilities
- Target's research and development capabilities
- Goodwill, brands and other intangible assets
- Opportunity of sharing overheads.

Methods for valuing businesses may be divided into two broad categories: income based valuations and asset based valuations.

Income based valuation methods

The more common income based valuation methods are:

- Exit price earnings ratio method – This method seeks to capitalise the net present value (NPV) of future earnings streams by applying a suitable exit price earnings (P/E) ratio to an estimate of maintainable earnings. Therefore, it will reflect the rate of growth and degree of volatility in the earnings stream. The maintainable earnings figure may be calculated after adjusting the accounting information for items of a non recurring nature. The exit P/E ratio will normally be derived by reference to transactions involving similar companies, and by assessment of the strengths and weaknesses of the business relative to similar businesses
- Application of a bid premium to a market share price – The quoted share price of a company represents the Stock Market's perception of the rate of growth and degree of volatility in the earnings of the company, together with other speculative factors including the possibility of take-over. However, the quoted price represents the cost of acquiring a small minority holding and does not reflect the added value of acquiring a significant holding or even complete control. Consequently, in order to determine a value for acquiring a significant part of the entire share capital of a company, a premium for control is usually added to the market price of the shares
- Discounted cash flow method – This method of valuation involves an assessment of the future cash flows from the business, to which a suitable discount rate is applied in order to calculate a net present value of those cash flows. The selection of

an appropriate discount factor and estimation of the timing and amount of future cash flows makes this method very subjective
- Dividend yield method – This method seeks to determine the flow of dividends anticipated to derive from an investment and to apply a discount rate to that flow in order to calculate a net present value of the dividend flow. However, this method is normally only of relevance when either a minority stake is involved or if there are restrictions on the remittance of earnings from the investment.

Asset based valuations

The main asset based valuation method is:
- Net asset value method – An asset based valuation typically places a value on a business by reference to the market value of its assets less its liabilities. This method of valuation is most suitable for valuing an asset based business such as a property investment company. However, the principal drawback with this method of valuation is that, in normal circumstances, it does not take account of the future earnings potential of the business. However, an asset based valuation does provide a base value that is easily determined by reference to balance sheet information, including recent valuations of key assets.

Disposals

A company may choose to dispose of a business unit as part of its overall business strategy. It will then need to:
- Identify potential purchasers
- Invite those parties who express an interest to make an offer
- Negotiate further with a preferred offeror
- Agree terms for the sale of the business.

Invariably, the vendor will not wish it to be widely known that the sale of a business unit is intended. Consequently, the vendor will often appoint a financial adviser who will identify potential purchasers and, with the vendor's approval, make an approach to those parties on a 'no names' basis. Should the identified party be interested in the opportunity, the financial adviser will arrange for a confidentiality agreement to be signed. This provides the vendor with an indication of the potential purchaser's commitment to ensure that any additional information supplied remains confidential.

Management Buy-Outs and Buy-Ins

Management Buy-Outs (MBOs) and Management Buy-Ins (MBIs) are transactions in which a management team joins with financing institutions to buy a business from its existing owners. An MBO is carried out by the incumbent management team, whereas an MBI is promoted by external management. For this reason, MBIs are considered to be far riskier than MBOs, and hence are less common because the management team will not have the inside track on the strengths and weaknesses of the business.

The lending banks and institutions provide most of the finance required, in the form of debt and equity, with the intention of realising a significant return on their investment. The institutions will typically look for an exit for their investment within three to five years of the buyout.

The structure of the finance provided by the institutions sometimes incorporates incentives for management over and above their initial equity stake. These incentives usually take the form of an equity 'ratchet' that enables management's equity stake to increase if certain specified targets are exceeded. These targets would normally be related to profit or cash flow performance and/or the exit value of the business.

The leverage effect

MBOs and MBIs work on the principle of leverage, or gearing. When a company is leveraged, any increase in the value of the business as a whole gives rise to a proportionately greater increase in the value of the shares in that business since the economic value of the debt remains constant. Naturally, gearing also carries with it a degree of risk for shareholders; the higher the level of gearing, the greater the risk that the value of the business will fall below the level of the debt. The shareholders would assess this risk at the outset and base their required investment return on this assessment.

The benefits of leverage allow MBOs and MBIs to be structured so that management teams can achieve significant gains from the transaction for a relatively small initial investment. At the outset, management will purchase a substantial percentage of the controlling equity in the business, usually for a small or nominal consideration. Then, if the acquisition debt is repaid as planned, a significant part of the value of the business will accrue to management.

Characteristics of a successful MBO/MBI business

A strong management team is particularly important for the success of an MBO or MBI. The management team will need to convince financing institutions that it is capable of managing the business in an independent environment.

In addition to management, financial stability is obviously critical to the success of the MBO or MBI. One definition of a successful MBO that is sometimes used is that it is 'the purchase of predictable cash flows at an economic price'. The key feature of this definition is that it refers to cash flow rather than profitability. Although profits will eventually convert into cash flow, the need to reduce the initial high level of borrowings inherent in MBOs and MBIs is such that the generation of cash is of paramount importance.

Of equal significance is that the cash flow should be reasonably predictable, that is, dependable, thereby providing comfort that interest and debt repayments will continue to be met. The greater the volatility in cash flows the greater the risk that a business will be unable to meet its financing obligations in any given period.

Venture capital

Venture capital may be defined as the provision of equity finance to companies that do not have ready access to public markets in order to fund start-ups, business expansion programmes and acquisitions. The venture capital industry in the UK has developed dramatically since it started in the early 1970s and now invests in excess of £1 billion each year.

The industry has its own association – The British Venture Capital Association (BVCA) – to which some 120 firms belong. BVCA members include:

- Independent companies with institutionally backed funds under management
- The unquoted equity interests of major investment institutions
- Business Expansion Scheme fund managers
- Government related bodies directly involved in the provision of equity finance for growing businesses.

Investment activity

In 1991, BVCA members invested in 1,196 companies in the UK. By investment type, these were:

	% of total number financed	% of total value financed
Start-ups & early stage investments	22	6
Expansion investments	55	39
MBOs and MBIs	23	55

Source: BVCA

Over 20 per cent of all companies financed were in technology related businesses, though consumer related businesses continued to be the most popular sector.

Sources of venture capital

Entrepreneurs and businesses seeking venture capital finance can obtain that finance from different sources. For small amounts, particularly in a start-up situation, an entrepreneur can sometimes obtain finance from private individuals, though such individuals can be difficult to locate. For larger amounts, finance can be raised from the following institutional sources:

- Independent venture capital funds: These include 3i, Candover and Electra who all raise their own funds for investment
- Venture capital subsidiaries of larger organisations, who obtain their finance in whole or in part from their parent companies. These include CINVEN, Prudential Venture Managers and County NatWest Ventures
- Government bodies: These include the West Midlands Enterprise Board, the Scottish Development Agency and the Welsh Development Agency who all manage funds on behalf of the Government and local authorities
- Business Expansion Scheme (BES) funds: These funds offer significant tax benefits to individual investors. Because BES funds are restricted in the size of investment that can be made in a business, they encourage investment in smaller businesses. In addition, once invested, the funds are effectively locked in for five years, because of the potential loss of tax relief if they are realised before this.

What do venture capitalists look for?

The reward for a venture capital fund lies in the growth of the businesses in which it invests. Consequently, the characteristics that a venture capitalist will look for in an investee company include:

- An experienced and effective management team
- Dependable cash flows

- A market where the company can gain a protected position
- A strong product.

Venture capitalists view the strength of the management team as the most important of these factors. It is primarily the management team that they are backing and consequently they must be comfortable that the team will be capable of managing the business in an independent environment.

The return that venture capitalists seek for their investment varies considerably. The fundamental principle that risk needs to be matched by return is applied by venture capitalists as much as by any other investor. Based on the type of the investment and the venture capitalists' views of the risks associated with the investment, a venture capital fund will seek returns of between 25 and 45 per cent per annum. The major element of this return is derived from the capital gain arising on the disposal of the venture capitalists' equity stake once an appropriate exit can be arranged.

Venture capitalists are not passive investors; they will require certain rights in order to monitor and protect their investment. A key requirement in this regard will be the ability to appoint a non-executive director of their choice.

Treasury

The treasury function of any entity (for example, a company, bank, local authority) has two essential roles:

- To manage liquidity, by ensuring that the entity is able to borrow the funds it needs to meet its liabilities as they fall due, and by placing surplus funds on deposit to earn interest income
- To monitor, and maintain within acceptable levels, the entity's exposure to movements in currency exchange rates and interest rates.

The treasury of a bank usually has two further responsibilities:

- To trade (buy and sell) foreign exchange, money market instruments and other risk management products for profit
- To service the needs of corporate customers for treasury products.

Although treasuries vary considerably in size and sophistication, they are all active to some extent in arranging transactions involving foreign exchanges, money market instruments and other risk management products in order to fulfil their defined role.

Foreign exchange

If there were a single world-wide currency, there would be no need for foreign exchange markets. All payments and receipts would be made in the same currency. However, in any international transaction, at least one party will be dealing in a foreign currency. The foreign exchange markets thus allow the parties to convert foreign currency cash flows into their own home currencies.

For example, a British importer purchasing machinery from the US for sale in the UK might have to pay the American manufacturer of the machinery in dollars. The importer would therefore sell his sterling sales receipts and purchase dollars in order to pay the manufacturer.

Exchange rates

The rate of exchange determines how many units of one currency are bought or sold in return for one unit of another currency. Exchange rates are available from a number of sources, the most common being the Financial Times, Reuters and Telerate. Rates are quoted for a number of currencies, usually for purchase or sale of sterling or US dollars. For example, dollar/sterling exchange rates may be quoted as follows:

		------- Forward rates ------		
	Spot	**30 day**	**90 day**	**180 day**
US$ per £	1.6955	1.6971	1.7010	1.7095

Spot market

The spot rate is the exchange rate for immediate delivery, payment usually taking place two days hence. Thus, if the importer required US$500,000 to pay his US supplier immediately, he would undertake a spot transaction and sell £294,898.26 at the spot rate, purchasing US$500,000 in exchange.

Forward market

It is also possible to buy and sell currency for future delivery, usually in one, three or six months' time. This is known as the forward foreign exchange market. The forward market is used when it is known that foreign currency will be received or paid at a future date. By buying or selling currency forward, the exchange rate is fixed, removing the possibility of loss caused by subsequent fluctuation in the exchange rate. However, the possibility of profiting from subsequent fluctuations in the exchange rate is also removed.

Thus, if the importer knows he will need another US$500,000 in six months' time, he may enter into a six month forward contract. The forward rate in this case is the rate at which he will buy dollars and sell sterling in six months when the dollars are required (that is, £1.00 = US$1.7095). In this case the importer will have to sell £292,483.18 and purchase US$500,000.

The forward rate may be calculated by comparing the interest rates for the specified period in each currency. Based on the law of arbitrage, the market is indifferent between buying $500,000 now and investing it for six months, or investing the appropriate amount of sterling for six months and selling it forward.

If dollar interest rates are 10 per cent, and sterling interest rates are 8.28 per cent, the six months forward rate is calculated as follows:

	US$		£
	500,000.00	@ 1.6955	294,898.26
Interest at 10% ($)	25,000.00		
Interest at 8.28% (£)			12,208.79
	525,000.00	=	307,107.05

Forward rate is $\frac{525{,}000.00}{307{,}107.05} = 1.7095$

In the example above, sterling is said to be trading at a forward premium relative to the dollar because forward sterling is more expensive than spot sterling in dollar terms. The forward premium is 1.7095 – 1.6955 = 0.014 (or 140 points).

Foreign exchange centres

The volume of international business transacted has grown enormously over recent years, as has the number and value of capital flows between nations. The resulting foreign exchange markets are the largest financial markets in the world.

However, the foreign exchange markets have no central exchange. All business is conducted over the telephone or telex. This lack of a central market and regulatory body means that reliable market data is scarce. However, three market surveys, undertaken by the Bank of England in 1986, 1989, and 1992, are summarised below.

The world's largest daily turnover of foreign exchange is centred on institutions based in London. The average volume of business in London is estimated to be US$303 billion per day (almost double the estimated US$187 billion in 1989 and more than treble the estimated US$90 billion in 1986). In addition, brokers in London are estimated to intermediate in transactions valued at US$12 billion per day between foreign institutions – which is not included in the US$303 billion.

The world's major centres for foreign exchange are as follows:

	Estimated daily turnover (US$ bn)		
	1992	**1989**	**1986**
London	303	187	90
New York	192	129	58
Tokyo	128	115	48
Switzerland	68	57	–
Singapore	–	55	–
Hong Kong	–	49	–
Paris	35	26	–
Frankfurt	–	–	–

Currency composition

As the following table shows, the foreign exchange trading centred on London is more diversified than in other major centres. Business in New York and Tokyo is concentrated mainly in transactions involving the domestic currency.

Currency composition (1989)
Percentage of principals' overall turnover

	London	Tokyo	New York
US$ / £	27	4	15
US$ / DM	22	10	33
US$ / Yen	15	72	25
US$ / Sw Fr	10	4	12
Other	26	10	15

Currency composition (1992)
Percentage of principals' overall turnover

	London	New York
US$ / £	19	9
US$ / DM	23	34
US$ / Yen	13	23
US$ / Sw fr	6	8
Other	39	26

Participants and the role of brokers

Most foreign exchange transactions are channelled through the world-wide market in which the banks trade with each other (the interbank market). All business is conducted by a network of central banks, commercial banks, multi-national corporations and brokers.

Central banks act to smooth exchange rate fluctuations by buying or selling large sums of currency. Commercial banks act as market makers – dealing in foreign exchange on their own account in a speculative manner. Multi-national corporations may be active in the markets in their own right, or may use the services of a broker. Brokers have traditionally played a special role in bringing buyers and sellers together in return for a commission payment. They still account for a large proportion of transactions in London although their significance has declined in recent years (34 per cent of deals in 1992, down from 38 per cent in 1989 and 43 per cent in 1986).

Money markets

The money market is the term used to describe the markets for liquid (often short term) financial instruments. In simple terms, they are the wholesale markets in which banks borrow or lend/invest money. They are an essential part of the international and domestic banking framework as they enable banks with excess funds to make profitable use of those funds by making them available, at a price, to those banks that have a shortage of funds.

The wholesale nature of the money markets means that single transactions can be for very large sums. Transactions are usually for sums of $1 million to $20 million, and transactions of $100 million and above are not uncommon. Some important features of these money markets are:

- The money markets are in fact a web of several interlinked markets in different financial instruments, including deposits, loans and certificates of deposit
- The markets are not located in any one place. They consist instead of an international network of dealers and brokers doing business over the telephone, telex, or by means of screen-based communications. They are therefore not restricted by location or by time zone
- The markets are not restricted to banks but include many large corporations, pension funds and other such bodies as active participants. In this section, only the role of banks is addressed
- The risk on some instruments is assumed to be zero because of the standing of the creditor (for example, US Treasury Bills), while on others the risk can be a significant consideration.

The interbank market

The interbank market is used both for raising short and medium term funding and for placing excess funds. The placements (otherwise known as loans and deposits) can be made on a 'call' basis whereby the money is repaid on demand, but are more normally on a fixed term basis. The terms range from one day (overnight) to five years, but the shorter maturities are the most common.

There are active interbank markets between the local banks in most countries (domestic markets). However, internationally, the most active interbank markets are in the Eurocurrency markets which are covered later in this chapter. Deposits in these markets are priced off the London Interbank Offered Rate (LIBOR), with each active participant in the market quoting a rate or margin over LIBOR at which they will place (lend) funds.

Other relevant rates are the London Interbank Bid Rate (LIBID) – the rate at which banks bid for deposits in the London interbank market – and LIMEAN – the average of LIBOR and LIBID. The spread between LIBOR and LIBID is usually of the order of an eighth of one per cent for banks of the highest credit-worthiness. The spread between these rates narrows or widens, according to the credit quality of the counterparty.

The Eurocurrency markets are international. Consequently, this interbank market is not confined to a single time zone and is a 24 hour market.

The participants

Money market activities are central to a bank's operations, since they provide:

- Access to short term funding
- A means of managing liquidity
- A benchmark to set interest rates on deposits and loans.

For many banks, an equally important function is utilising the money markets to generate additional profits by making markets in interest rate instruments, arbitraging between different markets or taking a view (speculating) on interest rate movements. Large corporations or other entities also use the money markets as a source of short term borrowing or investment.

There are two main reasons for using the money markets:

- If a bank is able to raise more from customer deposits than it can lend, the bank will use the money markets in order to:
  > invest its excess funds as profitably as possible
  > manage any interest rate exposure
  > manage liquidity, to ensure that funds are available to repay maturing assets, and that maturing liabilities can be replaced
  > trade an interest rate position
- If a bank has lent more than it can fund from its customer deposits, the bank will use the money markets in order to:
  > raise additional funding as cheaply as possible
  > manage any interest rate exposure
  > manage liquidity
  > trade an interest rate position.

Generally, a bank will use the money markets both for raising funds and for investing, to meet some or all of the following objectives:

- To maximise its use of capital by lending the maximum permitted by the capital/asset ratio
- To make profits from dealing (market making), from the spread between bid and offer interest rates

- To make profits from dealing, from taking interest rate positions
- To make arbitrage profits between the money markets and other related business activities
- To maintain a presence in the money markets and to build up a good reputation in those markets; most banks consider this an important aspect of money market activities, to ensure a ready source of short term funds at all times.

Currency, interest rate and liquidity risk

Institutions active in the treasury and capital markets face a number of complex risks, the most common being currency, interest rate and liquidity risk.

Currency risk

This is the risk that adverse movements in exchange rates will result in financial loss. This risk may arise in a variety of ways, apart from dealing activities. For example, where provisions are made against cash amounts receivable in currencies other than the home currency, it will be necessary to hedge these provisions in order to ensure that exchange losses are not incurred. Hedging involves taking contrary positions in the market so as to limit one's overall exposure.

For example, a UK bank has invested in a US dollar bond yielding 10 per cent, at an exchange rate of \$2 = £1. If the exchange rate moves to \$2 = £0.85, the bank has an unrealised loss of asset value in sterling terms.

The bank could have closed its exchange rate exposure by funding the US dollar bond by borrowing US dollars. In this case, any adverse effect of exchange rates on revaluing the asset would be offset by the effect of revaluing the liability. The exchange rate exposure then would only be on the net income (revenue from asset less funding cost) on the transaction.

Banks impose limits on their foreign exchange exposure (spot and forward) to ensure that any losses due to exchange rate movements are contained.

Interest rate risk

Interest rate risk is the risk that losses will be incurred through adverse movements in either the absolute level of interest rates or in the differential between two different interest rate bases.

The value of interest-bearing assets (for example, a bond or a deposit) changes as interest rates change. The relationship between asset value and interest rates is inverse; as interest rates rise, the value of an asset falls because it offers a lower return than the current market rate.

The level of interest rate exposure depends upon the extent of any mismatch in the timing of the interest rate re-fixings on assets and liabilities. For example, funding a six month deposit at 10 per cent with a one month inter-bank loan at 9.75 per cent creates an interest rate exposure. At the end of the first month, the loan must be repaid and new funding arranged. If interest rates have risen to 10.5 per cent, the cost of funding the asset (10.5 per cent) will be more than the return on the asset (10 per cent).

Interest rate risk should be controlled by means of limits. One commonly used limit is the mismatch limit, which sets the maximum amount by which liabilities repricing in any time period may exceed assets repricing in that time period, or vice versa. More complex forms of limits are also used – for example, based on duration (a mathematical expression of interest rate exposure as a single index).

Liquidity risk

Liquidity risk is the risk that an entity will be unable to meet its obligations as and when they fall due. For example, a bank that has lent long term and borrowed short term has high liquidity risk. If it cannot replace the short term borrowings when they have to be repaid, the bank will be insolvent. The management of liquidity risk involves securing a reasonable spread of maturities for assets and liabilities, and usually ensuring that there are more assets than liabilities maturing in the immediate future, perhaps seven days hence. The inter-bank market is used to adjust the short-term (up to about 18 months) liquidity of the bank.

Capital markets

The capital markets are the markets through which borrowers raise finance and investors invest funds in the form of bonds, loans or short-term paper. Banks and securities houses play a role in assisting capital flows and maintaining a liquid market.

Capital markets operations in banks and securities houses generally play one of three roles in the Euromarkets:

- Some capital markets operations act as investors. In other words, they maintain an investment portfolio on which they try to achieve the highest yield possible within given risk constraints
- Many capital markets operations play a part in the process of issuing bonds or paper. In effect, these operations intermediate between the issuers and the investors. This is a popular area of activity for capital markets players and typically generates fee income in return for the services provided

- A number of capital markets operations actively trade bonds and short term paper once they have been issued. This may be carried out as a service to the investors, particularly where the capital markets operation has been part of the issuing process. However, trading can also take place on an active basis, where the capital markets operation attempts to make profits from the price movements on the bonds.

History of the Euromarkets

One of the first Euromarkets was the Eurocurrency market. A Eurocurrency is a currency that is held outside its domestic country. For example, a US dollar bank account in London is a Eurodollar account. Similarly, a sterling bank account in France would be termed a Eurosterling account.

This 'Euro' prefix has been extended to cover other types of market with similar characteristics to the Eurocurrency markets. Thus the Euromarkets can now be defined as any market that consists of raising funds or issuing securities in a currency that is not the domestic currency of the country in which the funds are raised or the securities issued.

Eurobonds

The Eurobond market

A Eurobond is a bond issued and sold to investors outside the country in whose currency the bond is denominated. In contrast, a foreign bond is a security issued in a domestic market by a foreign borrower – for example, a French Franc bond issued by a UK or US company to French investors in French markets.

Eurobonds usually have a maturity in excess of 3 years, and have a total nominal value per issue in excess of US$100m.

It is generally accepted that the first Eurobond issue took place in 1963, when the Italian motorway company, Autostrade, launched a bond in the Euromarkets.

By 1969/70, the growth in the market was being impeded by the necessity for physical delivery of bonds and at this time both Euroclear and Cedel, the clearing houses, were established. The year 1970 also saw the issue of the first floating rate note (FRN). Up until this time, all Eurobonds issued had carried a fixed rate of interest.

Volumes in the Eurobond market continued to rise throughout the 1970s and the early 1980s, peaking in early 1986. However, at about this time there was a severe loss of confidence in one sector of the market – that for perpetual FRNs (which have no fixed maturity date). This caused a collapse in the perpetual FRN market and, to some extent, impacted on other sectors of the Eurobond market, leading to more depressed volumes in recent years.

Characteristics of a Eurobond

The general characteristics shared by most Eurobond issues are :

- They are long term instruments with maturities in excess of three, and up to 30, years
- The issues are usually unsecured, reflecting the credit quality of the borrowers
- The securities are negotiable instruments so that it is possible for investors to pass on title relatively easily. Eurobonds are issued in bearer form, such that the owner of the bond is whoever physically holds the piece of paper evidencing the debt. Thus Eurobonds are not registered in the same way as, for example, equities. This bearer status provides a degree of anonymity for the owner of the security which proves attractive to some investors
- Interest may be paid without the deduction for withholding tax. Because of the bearer nature of the instruments, interest is paid on presentation of a coupon attached to the side of a bond which gives the holder entitlement to an interest payment on certain dates. Thus when a Eurobond investor wishes to claim interest on the investment, the coupon is detached from the main bond and sent to the issuer who will then pay interest to whoever presents the coupon
- Eurobonds are issued in the Euromarkets and thus are typically outside the borrowers' domestic market.

The Eurobond market is international, but a significant proportion of all Eurobond activity is centred on London.

Eurobonds are normally listed on a stock exchange, although this is not a requirement. The listing is usually on either the Luxembourg Stock Exchange or The Stock Exchange in London. Listings are arranged to make issues more attractive to investors.

Issuing a Eurobond

Issuers in the Eurobond market invariably need to borrow such large sums of money that no single lender could contemplate providing the funds on its own account. The solution is to persuade a group of investors to group together and jointly make the necessary money available. The bond is first issued to a management and underwriting syndicate, which then sells the bonds to the ultimate investors.

Syndication is a way of spreading risk. It works in two stages. When a new issue is being launched, a group (a syndicate) of banks first agrees to 'underwrite' the bonds, ensuring that all of the bonds are taken up;

each member of the syndicate agrees to take a block onto its own books. In this way, a $100 million issue, for instance, could be split into five blocks of $20 million each. The second stage is put into effect when each of the syndicate of banks endeavours to sell its block of bonds to other banks, institutions or individuals.

Lead and co-managers

The issuer of a bond chooses a lead manager – a bank that arranges, manages and places the issue. The lead manager, sometimes in consultation with the issuer, can choose to invite a syndicate of banks to buy some of the bonds and help sell the remainder to other investors. Co-managers are thus invited to join the deal, each of whom agrees to take a substantial portion of the issue to sell to their investor clients. Quite often, there will be more than one lead manager.

Two or more lead managers may reflect the need for a geographical spread of placing power or indicate that the proceeds of the issue are to be swapped for another currency or interest rate structure.

One of the lead managers will 'run the books' for the issue. This is considered to be the plum job and essentially involves arranging the whole issue, sending out invitation telexes, and allotting bonds.

In a 'tombstone' announcement, placed in one of the financial newspapers or journals after an issue has been arranged, the lead managers and the co-managers will be listed. The bank running the books appears in the top left or top centre position while other institutions involved in the deal are listed either alphabetically or in descending order of involvement.

Lead managers may not be banks. British Petroleum, for example, has developed its own in-house financing capability and is fully capable of leading its own Eurobond issues.

Underwriters

The lead managers and co-managers act as 'underwriters' for the issue, taking on the risk of market prices changing before they have placed the bonds.

These banks may invite additional banks to act as sub-underwriters, so forming a larger underwriter group. A third group of banks may also be invited to join the issue as members of a 'selling group', but these institutions only receive a commission in respect of any bonds sold and do not act as underwriters. The co-managers and the underwriters are also members of the selling group.

Other types of Eurobond

Floating rate notes

A floating rate note (FRN) is a Eurobond carrying a rate of interest that is refixed periodically by reference to an interest rate bench mark – for example, six month LIBOR plus an eighth of one per cent. Variations include the following:

- Monthly fix and pay FRN: Interest is reset every month on a six month benchmark, and is paid to investors monthly
- Mis-match FRN: Interest is reset every month, but is paid every six months. Such FRNs provide a natural hedge for investors who are funding their bond investment on one month money
- Capped FRN: Carries a maximum rate of interest. For example, interest may reset every six months at six month LIBOR with a ceiling of, say, 10 per cent. Such bonds are effectively a package of a normal FRN and an interest rate option
- Mini-max FRN: Has both a maximum and a minimum rate of interest. Thus the FRN will reset its coupon to the current levels of interest every six months, provided that this is between the minimum and maximum rates
- Droplock FRNs: The bond will automatically convert into a fixed rate bond when short term interest rates fall below a specified level. Once the conversion has taken place, the bond does not convert back into an FRN, even if interest rates subsequently rise
- Inverse FRN: The coupon paid moves in an inverse relationship to movements in the benchmark interest rate. For example, if LIBOR increases, the coupon on an inverse FRN will decrease, and vice versa. Usually, the coupon is computed by deducting LIBOR from a fixed rate
- Perpetual FRN: An FRN with no fixed maturity. Such bonds work on the assumption that the bond can be sold at par at the interest reset date. Thus any investor wanting repayment can sell the bond to another investor at the interest reset date and obtain full repayment of the investment.

The theory behind perpetual FRNs presumes that there will always be a deep and liquid market for such bonds. Thus the market depends to a large extent upon confidence. When confidence in the market deteriorated in 1986, investors found that there were no buyers for their bonds and the rationale behind such issues collapsed.

Bonds with warrants

Warrants are separate instruments that are attached to bonds and are essentially options to buy either equity in the company or further bonds. Instead of paying a premium for such options, the investor accepts a lower return on the bond. In many instances, the warrants are 'stripped' from the bond and traded separately.

Equity warrants attached to the bond give investors the option to purchase equity in the company at a fixed price. Typically, this fixed price will be higher than the current market price of the company's equity. The expectation is that the market price will rise above the warrant price and thus give rise to a profit; it is this expectation that gives warrants their value.

It should be noted that bonds with equity warrants are different from convertibles. A convertible bond merely gives the holder the opportunity to convert debt finance (bonds) to equity finance (shares), but does not lead to the injection of new capital. In the case of an equity warrant, the investor has the right to purchase additional shares in the company – that is, to inject new capital into the company by making an investment of fresh funds.

Bond warrants give the investors the option to purchase further bonds at a predetermined price in the future. Eurobonds that are issued with warrants that allow the investor to purchase further bonds from the same issue have sometimes been referred to as 'bunny' bonds as such bonds have the ability to 'reproduce' very quickly.

Junk bonds

Junk bonds are high yielding bonds that became fashionable in the 1980s as a means of financing highly leveraged acquisitions, the high yield reflecting the risk associated with the bond. The junk bond market suffered a serious blow with the demise, in 1990, of Drexel Burnham Lambert – the company responsible for establishing the market – and has remained unpopular since.

Eurocommercial paper

Traditionally, short term finance has been provided directly by banks, through products such as overdrafts and acceptance facilities. Increasingly, corporate borrowers are also turning to the Euromarkets for short term finance. While products such as bonds and equities still dominate the Euromarkets, the commercial paper markets have grown quickly over the last few years as capital market participants have looked to diversify their product ranges.

Commercial paper is a short term note (debt instrument), issued under the umbrella of a medium term facility. Thus a commercial paper facility will be set up for, say, two to seven years and this facility will then be drawn down through the issue of a series of short term promissory notes whose maturities will vary from one month up to one year. As these promissory notes mature, the finance is maintained by issuing further notes.

For a borrower, a commercial paper facility carries the risk that the issue of more paper will become difficult or impossible if, for example, there is a major deterioration in the credit status of the issuer.

This risk may be mitigated by:

- Arranging underwriting for the term of the facility, by which a syndicate of banks agree to buy any paper which cannot be placed directly with investors
- Arranging a committed facility to provide funds in the event that the issue of notes is not a success. Such facilities, sometimes known as standby or swingline facilities, tend to cost less than a committed facility upon which the borrower intends to draw at some time. Since such swingline facilities will only be called upon in the event that the note issue is not a success, the likelihood of a bank being called upon to provide funds is somewhat less than in a straightforward committed facility and the commitment fee will reflect this.

Eurocommercial paper (ECP) is commercial paper issued in the Euromarkets. While not nearly so well established as either the Eurobond market or the US commercial paper market, the ECP market has grown rapidly in the past few years.

Distribution of Eurocommercial paper

In the ECP market, paper is typically distributed through the same mechanism used for bond distribution. This has the advantage of utilising established distribution networks.

Typically, two or three banks or investment houses are appointed to a dealership. These institutions buy the notes from the issuer at an agreed price and then sell these notes on to investors. Any difference between the price at which the dealers buy and sell represents remuneration for the dealers. While sole dealerships do exist, it is more usual to appoint two or three agents to ensure a good spread of potential investors and to encourage competition. It should be noted that, on occasions, dealers are not kept for the full term of the facility and, indeed, there have been a small number of cases in which companies have changed their dealers during the life of the facility.

From the perspective of the bank, commercial paper business provides fee income and, indeed, repeat fee income. With a Eurobond issue, there is only one fee as there is only one issue. With commercial paper, there are fees to be earned each time paper is issued. Commercial paper also provides the investment houses with a fuller product range when contacting their investor bases and helps maintain contact with the investor base at a time when there may not be a great deal of new issues activity in the Eurobond market.

Syndicated loans

A syndicated loan is a large (often over $100m) long term bank loan that is provided by a syndicate of banks rather than one lender. Interest rates on the loan generally relate to LIBOR or LIBID, depending on the credit rating of the borrower.

The loan is relatively flexible in that the borrower need not draw down the complete amount of the loan, but may borrow as much as is required up to a set limit. Interest is paid only on the amount outstanding, giving the loan an advantage over a bond issue, which would require that interest is paid on the full amount until the bond is repaid.

Syndicated loans were traditionally attractive to State borrowers who needed to raise large scale finance. However, their popularity has declined in recent years following a large number of defaults, deferrals and reschedulings, which has resulted in considerably higher risk ratings for most borrowers.

The arrangement of syndicated loans follows a similar pattern to other products in the Euromarkets – such as Eurobonds and Euro commercial paper – with a lead manager structure.

Instruments to manage risk

Over the last decade, a new range of financial products has evolved, known as derivatives. They are sometimes called off-balance sheet instruments because they are not accounted for on the balance sheet (though recent proposals from the Accounting Standards Board, if implemented, would change this). These products are widely used to manage currency and interest rate risk and now form an important component of treasury and capital markets operation.

The four most important groups of products are:

- Futures
- Forward rate agreements (FRAs)
- Swaps
- Options.

Financial futures

A financial future contract is an agreement to buy or sell a standard quantity of a specific financial instrument at a predetermined future date and at a price agreed between the parties on an organised exchange. There are no significant structural differences between futures contracts on interest rate instruments ('interest rate futures') and those on currencies ('currency futures').

Exchanges

The principal exchanges are:

- The Chicago Board of Trade (CBT)
- The International Monetary Market (IMM) of the Chicago Mercantile Exchange (CME)
- The New York Futures Exchange (NYFE)
- The London International Financial Futures Exchange (LIFFE).

Contracts are traded through brokers who usually clear and settle transactions on the exchange. If the clearing is executed through a different broker, then the broker through which the trade was made is called an agent broker.

The standardisation of contracts enables participants to buy and sell freely on the exchange where the contract is traded, with precise knowledge regarding the characteristics of the contracts being traded. Participants may offset equal numbers of identical bought and sold contracts (close out a position) without the need for further communication with the counterparties to the original transaction. This relieves the participant from the need to take or make delivery on the contracts.

Types of financial futures contract

Financial futures contracts are of three basic types:

- Interest rate futures
- Currency futures
- Stock index futures.

Interest rate futures are based on particular types of financial instruments, whose prices are dependent on interest rates. Currency futures are based upon certain internationally important currencies. Stock index futures are based on certain internationally recognised stock exchange indices.

Mechanics of a futures contract

The purchase or sale of a financial futures contract through an exchange is a commitment to make, or take, delivery of a specific financial instrument, or to perform a particular service, at a pre-determined date in the future, for which the price is established at the time of initial execution.

For example, the purchase of a June three month dollar contract commits the purchaser to make a deposit of $1,000,000 in June for three months at an agreed interest rate implicit in the price.

As the market price moves for a particular delivery date, holders of open future contracts (contracts that have not been closed out) will see corresponding profits and losses from their holdings. The standard nature of each futures contract makes such gains and losses easy to measure and monitor. Price movements are tracked in terms of minimum price fluctuations allowed by the exchange, which are referred to as 'ticks' and carry a definite value for each contract type.

For example, the price of a dollar contract is quoted on an index basis – that is, 100 minus the annual interest rate on a three month time deposit. Each tick represents $25, being interest at a rate of a hundredth of one per cent for three months on $1,000,000.

Uses of financial futures contracts

The two primary uses of financial futures are:

- Hedging
- Trading.

Hedging aims to reduce the risk of adverse movements in financial rates, by taking a position in a financial futures contract that offsets the existing or anticipated position in the cash market. For example, a bank can lock into a current lending rate for cash that it knows will be available for long term investment in three months' time by buying the appropriate futures contract. It is important to note that if a futures contract is used to hedge a position, then a party is 'locked in' to the rate, no matter which way the actual rate moves. Protection against adverse movement in rates, without eliminating the advantages of favourable movements, may be obtained using options (see below).

Trading in financial futures contracts enables organisations or individuals to seek profits from rises or falls in interest rates or exchange rates, without necessarily having to buy or sell the underlying financial instrument or currency.

Both hedgers and traders are necessary for the efficient operation of the futures markets. Traders are prepared to assume the risks that hedgers seek to avoid, thus providing the market with the necessary liquidity.

Margin trading

A futures contract is executed by depositing a specified 'initial margin' with a futures broker. At the end of each trading day, any changes in market value are charged or credited to the individual customer accounts. These changes are referred to as 'variation margin'. If the customer's account increases above the initial margin level, he may withdraw the excess amount in cash. Alternatively, if the customer's account falls below the specified 'maintenance margin' (an amount slightly less than the initial margin), the customer is subject to a 'margin call' and is required to post an additional amount of cash or government securities to bring the account balance back up to the initial margin level.

The levels of initial and maintenance margin requirements are prescribed by the exchange. Margin requirements are in part a function of the historical volatility of prices. They may be as little as 0.1 per cent of the face value of the contract (for example, $1,000 for a $1 million Treasury Bill futures contract), thereby making futures contracts highly leveraged, volatile, risky instruments.

Forward rate agreements

A forward rate agreement (also referred to as future or fixed rate agreement) is an agreement between two parties, fixing the interest rate for a period commencing on a future date, normally within the next 12 months. No commitment is made by either party to lend or borrow funds – the only commitment is to pay or receive an interest differential based upon a notional principal amount. FRAs are used to modify interest rate risk.

The following are essential features of an FRA:

- The parties do not exchange or pay the principal amount – it is notional only
- The contract is settled by means of a single payment, representing the difference between the interest rate stated in the contract and the market interest rates for the period specified in the contract
- The buyer and the seller of the FRA agree transactions either directly or via a broker, rather than through a formal market place, such as an exchange.

Most transactions undertaken in the London market are settled in accordance with the British Bankers' Association terms (FRABBA terms). Standardised terms have also been developed in other markets where FRAs are commonly used. Standard terms remove the need for lengthy legal documentation and complex negotiations. This is because the FRABBA and other similar terms specify the methods to be applied in determining interest rates at the settlement date, how to calculate the settlement sum and the meaning of certain important phrases used in the FRA markets.

The mechanics of a transaction

The following are the steps involved in a forward rate agreement transaction:

- A transaction may be initiated either by a buyer or the seller of the FRA asking the writer (normally a bank) of the FRA for a quote
- The quote will take the form of a fixed interest rate for the relevant period

- A contract will be agreed, normally referring to FRABBA terms, and evidenced by exchange of confirmations. The contract will specify the period, the notional principal, the agreed rate and the market rate (for example, three month LIBOR) to be used as a reference at settlement
- At the settlement date (which is the start of the period being covered), one single payment changes hands to fulfil the contract. This is calculated using the FRABBA settlement formula or any other formula agreed at the outset of the contract. The FRABBA formula is:

$$S = \frac{(L - R) \times D \times A}{(B \times 100) + (L \times D)}$$

Where:
S = Settlement amount
L = Prevailing market rate, as defined
R = FRA or contract rate
D = Number of days of notional loan or deposit in contract period
A = Notional principal or contract amount
B = Interest basis (360 days, or 365 in the case of Sterling)

An example of an FRA contract

The buyer of a $5 million two months against five months FRA contract asks his bankers for a quote. The contract will cover the three month period starting in two months' time and ending in five months' time.

The bank would construct the quote as follows:

Market rate for two month deposits	9.5%
Number of days in two month period	61
Market rate for five month deposits	10.5%
Number of days in five month period	152

The forward rate for the two against five period (that is, the three month period starting in two months' time) is the three month rate implied by the above data calculated as follows:

Interest earned in two months:

$$\$5{,}000{,}000 \times \frac{61}{360} \times 9.5\% = \$80{,}486$$

Interest earned in five months:

$$\$5{,}000{,}000 \times \frac{152}{360} \times 10.5\% = \$221{,}667$$

The implied interest rate for the last three months or 91 days can be calculated as follows:

$$\frac{\$221{,}667 - \$80{,}486}{\$5{,}080{,}486} \times \frac{360}{91} \times 100 = 11\%$$

That is interest earned in the last three months expressed as an annualised percentage of the principal outstanding at month 2.

At settlement date, that is, after two months, the market rate is 12 per cent. The buyer is, however, protected against this rise in interest rates over the FRA rate of 11 per cent and will receive a payment from the bank as follows:

$$\$5{,}000{,}000 \times (12\% - 11\%) \times \frac{91}{360} = \$12{,}639$$

Because the payment arises at the start of the three month period this sum must be discounted at the current market rates thereby assuming that the purchaser of the FRA can reinvest such sum at such rates. Accordingly, the payment is reduced to:

$$\$12{,}639 \times \frac{1}{1 + (12\% \times \frac{91}{360})} = \$12{,}267$$

The same result would be obtained by using the FRABBA settlement formula above:

$$\frac{(12 - 11) \times 91 \times 5{,}000{,}000}{(360 \times 100) + (12 \times 91)} = \$12{,}267$$

While there is a large market in FRAs in London, the instrument is less popular in the United States, mainly because it is difficult to develop a large market when there are a large number of different contracts. Because FRAs are tailored to specific customer requirements, each contract is slightly different. In order to develop a deep liquid market in an instrument, there needs to be a degree of standardisation.

Swaps

A swap is an agreement between two parties to exchange one set of cash flows for another. Swaps result in the economic exchange of interest rates, currencies, basis rates or any combination thereof. Swaps are simply a highly structured series of cash flows.

In the case of an interest rate swap, no exchange of principal takes place. Instead, 'interest' payments are made on a notional principal amount.

In a currency swap, the principal sum is always exchanged at the end of the swap period and may, depending on the needs of the counter parties, be exchanged at the start of the swap period.

Interest rate swaps
A is a 'triple A' rated company (that is, a company with a very high credit standing). Company A requires floating rate debt but is also able to borrow relatively cheaply in the fixed rate market. B is a less highly rated company, which finds access to the fixed rate market to be difficult and/or very expensive. In general, the credit rating of the borrower is of greater significance to a fixed rate lender than for a floating rate lender.

The market rates available to A and B are as follows:

	A	**B**	**Advantage of A over B**
Floating	LIBOR + 0.25%	LIBOR + 1%	0.75%
Fixed	10%	12%	2%

Both parties raise finance as they normally would in the markets in which they have a relative advantage, A and B then separately enter into a swap with a bank as set out in the diagram below.

On each interest date, A would pay to, or receive from, the bank the difference between 10.25 per cent and LIBOR. B would receive from, or pay to, the bank the difference between LIBOR and 10.75 per cent.

A pays	(10%)	Bank receives	LIBOR%	B pays	(LIBOR + 1%)
A receives	10.25%	Bank receives	10.75%	B receives	LIBOR
A pays	(LIBOR)	Bank pays	(LIBOR%)	B pays	(10.75%)
Net cost	(LIBOR-0.25%)	Bank pays	(10.25%)	Net cost	(11.75%)
Market rate	LIBOR+0.25%			Market rate	12%
Saving to A	0.5%	Profit to bank	0.5%	Saving to B	0.25%

This arrangement is of benefit to both A and B as it exploits the comparative advantage of A over B in the fixed rate market. A is able to raise funds more cheaply than B in both markets, but it has a greater advantage in the fixed rate market – the market which it does not want to use.

When the swap market first evolved, transactions were arranged by banks between two specific parties, as in the above example. As the market has developed, liquidity has improved, and banks are now active traders of swaps, either managing a hedged swap portfolio or carrying unmatched swaps as part of their own interest rate position.

Another form of interest rate swap is the basis swap, which swaps two floating rate cash flows, though each is related to a different benchmark – for example, $LIBOR and US$ Prime rate.

Currency swaps

A currency swap involves an exchange of interest liabilities in different currencies. It usually consists of three stages:

- An initial exchange of the principal amounts. This does not always form part of the swap agreement as a similar effect can be obtained by using the spot foreign exchange market
- Continuing exchange of interest payments during the term of the swap. This, in effect, represents a series of forward foreign exchange contracts during the term of the swap contract
- Re-exchange of principal on maturity.

A more complex version of a currency swap is a currency coupon swap, which swaps a fixed or floating rate interest payment in one currency for a floating rate payment in another currency. These swaps are also known as combined interest rate and currency swap 'circuses'.

Non-generic swaps

Swaps that are not standard interest rate or currency swaps are often referred to as non-generic swaps. Examples are:

- Amortising swaps: The notional principal alters over the term of the swap
- Forward swaps: The swap is arranged to run from some future date
- Swaptions: Options on swaps, which give the buyer of the swaption the right (but not the obligation) to enter into a swap agreement for a predetermined term, notional principal and interest rates
- Callable swaps: These are similar to swaptions, but instead give the swap counterparty the right to terminate the swap
- Arranger swaps: A swap transaction that involves a complex combination of swaps and other transactions (such as foreign exchange contracts, futures, money market transactions and bond positions).

Use of swaps

Swaps can be used for two different categories of transaction:

- Hedging
- Position taking.

Hedging includes the situation where a company has either new or existing debt and wishes to change the interest rate or currency risk profile of that debt. Similarly, swaps provide a method of managing the return on an investment, by means of asset swaps.

Position taking is when swaps are used to create an overall interest rate or currency position. In such cases, it is likely that the bank will wish to move in and out of the swap position. This can be achieved by the following methods which are, in essence, very similar:

- Entering into a new, off-setting, swap or other position
- Cancelling the swap. The swap cancellation normally entails the payment of a fee to or from the swap counter-party.

Legal framework

All swaps are subject to legal agreements between the various parties. The market place has developed various frameworks within which these contracts are determined.

The International Swap Dealers Association (ISDA) code of standard wording, assumptions and provisions for swaps provides a comprehensive set of definitions and provisions designed to make the work of professional traders, their counsel and their support staff simpler by acting as a common framework for communication between market participants. It addresses such matters as how to determine payments due to or from the swap parties, whether payments are to be made net or gross, right to terminate, how to establish amounts due upon early termination, governing law, taxation matters, etc.

In the UK, use of the British Bankers' Association interest rate swap terms (BBAIRS terms) is normal market practice. BBAIRS terms apply to inter-bank transactions of maturity of up to two years and cover single currency fixed floating swaps and cross currency swaps (fixed to fixed, fixed to USD floating, floating to floating). These terms are not prescriptive and banks are free to deal with counterparties on other terms or to use these terms for other forms of swaps.

The legal position regarding swaps entered into by UK local authorities was recently clarified by a Supreme Court ruling which stated that swap contracts entered into by these counterparties are *ultra vires* and hence invalid. This has meant that local authorities can refuse to honour outstanding obligations under such agreements.

Options

Options are in many ways the most complex instruments to deal with. However, they are not new. Options on tulip bulbs were generally traded in Amsterdam in the 18th century. Nonetheless, they do cause a great deal of confusion, particularly because of the one-sided nature of the risk.

An option confers on a buyer the *right* but not the *obligation* to buy (call), or sell (put), a *specific* quantity of a *specific* underlying asset or instrument at a *fixed price* at or before a *future* date. In return for this right, the buyer pays to the seller a *premium*.

Options can relate to many different types of instruments including equity stock, fixed interest rate instruments, interest rates themselves, currencies and commodities. This section concentrates on those relating to interest rate instruments and currencies.

Terminology

Terminology used in relation to options includes:

- Put: An option relating to the sale of an underlying instrument
- Call: An option relating to the purchase of an underlying instrument
- Strike (or Exercise) Price: The price at which the option may be exercised
- Premium: The amount which is paid by the buyer to the seller (or writer) of the option in return for the option right
- Expiration date: The date on which the option ceases to be exercisable
- 'In the money': An option which has intrinsic value. That is, the immediate use of the option will enable a holder to obtain something of value. For example, the holder of a call option to buy a US dollar treasury stock at US$100 could exercise the option, and if the current market price is US$102, would realise US$2. The option is therefore said to be 'in the money'. Similarly, if the current market price is US$100, the option is said to be 'at the money', and conversely if the market price is US$98 the option does not have any intrinsic value and is 'out of the money'

European options are exercisable only at the expiry of the option. Conversely, an American option is exercisable at any point during its life.

Exchange traded options are traded on a recognised exchange in standard amounts – for example, the Philadelphia Stock Exchange, the Chicago Board Options Exchange or LIFFE in London. 'Over the counter' (OTC) options are entered into between a bank or other provider and its customer.

Profit characteristics

As might be expected from the one sided nature of the obligation, the profit characteristics of options are asymmetrical. The profit characteristics for the buyer of a call option are:

- The maximum loss is the amount of the premium paid. This is constant for any price of the underlying instrument below the strike price

- As the price moves above the strike price, the option gradually acquires value and the potential profit is unlimited.

By contrast, for the writer of a call option, the maximum amount of money that can be made is fixed, but the loss potential is infinite.

Buy a call option

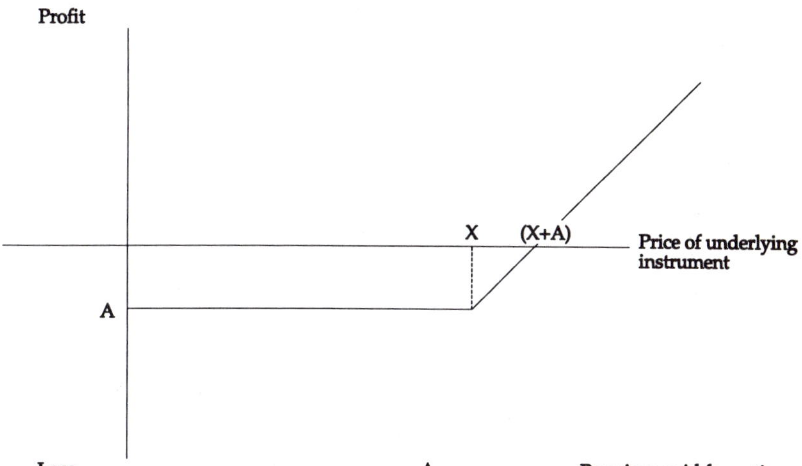

A	=	Premium paid for option
X	=	Strike price
(X+A)	=	Price of underlying security at which option strategy becomes profitable

For the buyer of a put option, the maximum loss is the premium paid. This is constant for any price of the underlying instrument above the strike price. As the price falls below the strike price, the put option acquires value and the potential profit is unlimited down to a price of the underlying instrument of zero.

Buy a put option

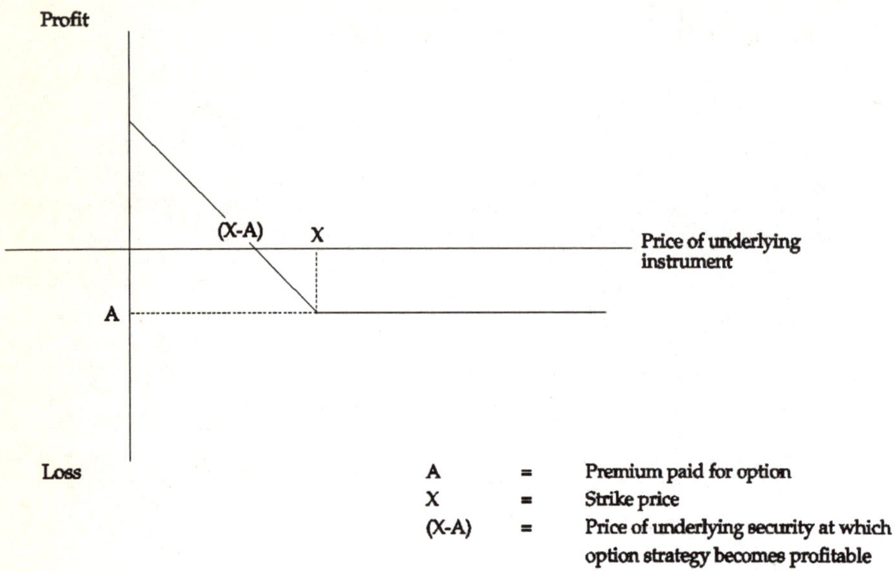

By contrast, the profit profile of the writer of a put option is such that the maximum income that can be earned is fixed, and equal to the premium received, but the potential loss is unlimited.

Business taxation

Business activities can be carried out through a variety of legal entities, the main ones being companies and branches, sole traders and partnerships. The way in which each of these entities is taxed will vary (though many of the basic rules are fundamentally the same) and this will have an impact on how and why each entity is used by its owner as a vehicle to carry out a business.

The principal taxes that are relevant to the taxation of business profits in the UK are:

- Corporation tax (applies to both the income and capital gains of companies)
- Income tax (applies to the income of sole traders and partnerships)
- Capital gains tax (applies to the capital gains of sole traders and partnerships)
- Petroleum revenue tax (a special tax applying to the profits from oil exploration in the North Sea and UK mainland).

In addition to these taxes on business profits, businesses may also be affected by other taxes that, generally, apply more to particular transactions than to profits earned. These taxes include:

- Value Added Tax
- Customs and Excise Duties
- Stamp Duty
- Uniform Business Rates.

Legislative framework

The statutory provisions governing the taxation of businesses in the UK are amended, or expanded, each year by a Finance Act passed by Parliament (occasionally, most often where there is an election or change of Government, there may be two Finance Acts). The tax legislation distinguishes the UK from the rest of the world and, for most tax purposes, the UK includes England, Scotland, Wales, Northern Ireland and the Scilly Isles – but not the Isle of Man or the Channel Isles.

In the past, the Finance Acts have normally been passed around July each year, following the Chancellor's Budget in March. In March 1992, the Chancellor announced that this pattern was to be revised so that the Budget Speech would be given each year in November or December (starting in 1993) at the same time as the Government's Autumn Statement, which sets out the following year's spending plans. As a result, the timetable for the passage of each year's Finance Act will be brought forward by three months. This new arrangement will mean that the publication and discussion of the Government's spending plans will occur at the same time as the consideration of how those plans will be financed.

Because each year's Finance Act will make changes to the existing legislation, over time the legislation can get fragmented and disorganised, with legislation being spread across a number of Finance Acts. The legislation is therefore consolidated periodically, to bring together pieces of legislation affecting a single area or topic from the various preceding Finance Acts into a single consolidation Act.

The bulk of the legislation covering the taxation of income for all types of business is currently embodied in the Income and Corporation Taxes Act, 1988, supplemented by subsequent Finance Acts. Other consolidation Acts cover areas such as:

- Capital gains (Taxation of Chargeable Gains Act, 1992)
- Capital allowances (Capital Allowances Act, 1990)
- Value added tax (Value Added Tax Act, 1983)
- Administration (Taxes Management Act, 1970).

In addition to the framework set out by statute, a considerable body of case law, derived from the decisions of the Courts, exists. These Court cases arise where a taxpayer and the Inland Revenue have been unable to agree on the correct interpretation of the tax legislation and seek a decision in the Courts. The decisions of the highest Court, the House of Lords, acting in its judicial capacity, are binding on the lower Courts and, similarly, the decisions of the Court of Appeal are binding on the High Court. The Inland Revenue has also issued extra-statutory concessions and statements of practice that assist in the interpretation of the tax legislation.

Concepts of Income Tax

The structure of most UK taxation is based on concepts of income tax that have grown up over a long period. Many aspects of UK taxation appear somewhat convoluted and unnecessarily complex, reflecting historical features that have been difficult to change (there will always be winners and losers in making any transition) but which are now rather anachronistic.

Schedules and Cases

One of these features is the pattern of Schedules and Cases that form the bones of the UK tax regime. These have their origins in the period of the Napoleonic wars when income tax was first introduced. So that wealthy individuals of the time would not have to disclose the whole of their income to civil servants, the schedular system was created whereby the income from different sources was separately computed and assessed to tax. This system is retained today in the structure of modern income tax and also corporation tax, which adopts income tax rules as its foundation.

The categories into which income is classified for income tax and corporation tax purposes are set out in five schedules, some of which are further divided into cases, as follows:

- Schedule A: Net rental income from real estate in the UK
- Schedule C: Public revenue dividends payable in the UK
- Schedule D:
  Case I – Profits of a trade
  Case II – Profits of a profession or vocation
  Case III – Receipts of interest, annuities and other annual payments
  Case IV – Income from foreign securities
  Case V – Income from foreign possessions (including trades carried on wholly overseas)
  Case VI – Miscellaneous income
- Schedule E: Income from employment, including occupational pensions
- Schedule F: Dividends and other distributions from UK companies.

Schedule B related to the taxation of woodlands but has now been abolished.

Fiscal and financial years

Historically, the financial year in the UK began on Lady Day – 25 March. In 1752, this was changed with the revision of the calendar and the start of the financial year became 6 April. The year from 6 April to the following 5 April is now the period for which tax is calculated for individuals and is called the fiscal year. Thus fiscal year 1993/94 means the tax year starting on 6 April 1993 and ending on 5 April 1994. Each year's Budget sets the rates of taxation, and the various reliefs available, for individuals assessed to income tax and capital gains tax.

For its own budgetary purposes, the Government uses a financial year that commences on 1 April and ends on the following 31 March. Financial years are generally known by a single year – thus financial year 1993 is the year starting 1 April 1993 and ending on 31 March 1994. The rate of corporation tax and the reliefs relevant to companies are set by reference to financial years rather than the fiscal years used for individuals.

Tax residence

The liability to UK taxation is initially determined by an individual's, or company's, residence.

Company residence was not statutorily defined in the UK tax legislation prior to 15 March 1988. Before then, it was case law that established the general principle that a company is resident in the UK if its 'central management and control' is exercised there and further case law has grown up examining what is meant by 'central management and control'. From 15 March 1988, a second statutory test of residence was introduced based on country of incorporation – namely, that any company incorporated in the UK is presumed to be UK resident. (However, companies incorporated in the UK prior to 15 March 1988, which were not already resident under the central management and control test, generally were not treated as UK resident in most cases until 15 March 1993.)

As companies will be considered to be resident in the UK under either the central management and control test or the incorporation test, companies may be dual resident (depending on the definition of residence in the overseas country). This may occur if, for example, a company is incorporated in the UK but operates in another country, where the nature of its activities is such that it is considered resident in that country.

The determination of UK residence for individuals depends upon physical presence. An individual is always treated as resident in the United Kingdom if he is physically present in the country for a period, or periods, that in total exceed six months in any fiscal year (the year to 5 April). In certain circumstances, an individual may be treated as resident in the United Kingdom if his physical presence here in a particular tax year is for a shorter period – for example, if he has spent an average of three months or more per year in the UK over a period of four years.

A UK resident company is subject to corporation tax on its world-wide income and capital gains. This contrasts with a non-UK resident company, which is subject to corporation tax only on the trading profits and capital gains arising from a trade carried on in the UK through a branch or agency and on investment income arising from branch property.

As for companies, UK resident individuals and partnerships are subject to income tax on their world-wide income and capital gains (special rules apply for individuals domiciled outside, but resident in, the UK). Non-resident individuals and partnerships are subject to income tax only from income arising in the UK.

Capital gains tax is chargeable on gains arising on all assets, wherever they are situated, for UK resident companies, individuals and partnerships. For non-residents, gains are chargeable where assets are used in connection with a branch or trade here.

EC harmonisation

As a member of the European Community, the United Kingdom has agreed to the principle of a Single European market involving the abolition of any remaining physical, fiscal and technical barriers to trade within the Community. The UK is therefore committed to the long term aim of tax harmonisation within the Community. Varying degrees of harmonisation on the different UK taxes have been achieved to date.

Harmonisation of corporation tax on the basis of a common imputation system has been proposed but progress towards achieving this has been slow. However, two EC directives took effect within the UK on 1 January 1992, concerning the abolition of withholding tax on certain dividend payments within the EC and the deferral of tax on capital gains on defined cross-border mergers or reorganisations within the Community. As yet, neither of these directives has been fully implemented in all countries of the EC.

Harmonisation of VAT is being achieved slowly through directives issued by the Council of Ministers. Presently all member states have to apply a minimum rate of VAT (although actual rates applied vary from country to country) and, since 1 January 1993, all customs formalities at intra-community borders were virtually abolished.

Administration

Corporation Tax

Corporation tax is charged on companies by means of an assessment raised by an Inspector of Taxes. The normal due date for payment of corporation tax is nine months after the accounting period end.

If no tax computation has been submitted prior to this date, the Inspector will raise an estimated assessment, based on the previous year's profits. Such an assessment will become final and conclusive unless a written appeal is made to the Inspector of Taxes within 30 days of the date of issue. Application to postpone any tax charged in excess of the estimated final liability may also be made by the taxpayer.

Tax is normally payable on the later of the due date or 30 days after the issue of an assessment (or the Inspector's agreement of postponement application, if applicable). Interest on overdue tax will normally only be charged from the table date (six months after the due date), unless information has been withheld from the Inspector of Taxes, when interest may run from the due date.

Actual corporation tax liabilities will be determined when the tax computations have been agreed. If agreement cannot be reached with the local Inspector of Taxes, the case may be heard by the Commissioners for Income Tax (a body of independent arbitrators who act as the first stage in the litigation process).

There is an obligation on the taxpayer to provide details of income to the Inland Revenue and to pay the appropriate tax by the due date, otherwise the Inland Revenue has the authority to levy penalties and interest on overdue tax, which may be substantial.

'Pay and File'

The UK is introducing a 'Pay and File' system which applies to accounting periods ending on or after 1 October 1993. Companies will be required to estimate and pay their corporation tax nine months after the accounting period end, whether an assessment has been issued or not and returns will be due within one year from the end of the accounting period. Automatic penalties will be imposed, if these conditions are not fulfilled.

Income Tax

In general, the compliance requirements for individuals are similar to those for companies. However, the normal due date on which income tax is payable is half on 1 January in the fiscal year and half on the following 1 July.

These dates, however, apply mainly to self-employed individuals and not employees, whose income is usually subject to income tax under the Pay As You Earn (PAYE) system.

Value Added Tax

Businesses and individuals must be registered for VAT, if their taxable supplies exceed, or are expected to exceed, £37,600 per annum. VAT returns must normally be made on a quarterly basis (large companies were required to make monthly payments on account from late 1992) but, if the company would normally be in a repayment situation, it may apply for monthly returns. Customs and Excise have extensive powers to ensure that registration has taken place, returns have been submitted on time, and the correct amount of tax has been paid.

Taxation of companies

Companies and shareholders

There are, broadly, two systems of company taxation – the 'classical' system and the 'imputation' system. Under the classical system, the shareholders are taxed separately from the company. The company will be taxed once when earning the profits out of which it pays dividends and the shareholders also will be subject to income tax on those profits in the form of the dividends they receive from the company. No account is taken of any tax that has already been levied on those profits in the hands of the company.

However, under an imputation system, shareholders are imputed to receive a tax credit with their dividend reflecting the tax that the company has already paid on those profits.

Since 1973, the UK has operated an imputation system; before that, the classical system applied. Companies are now subject to a flat rate of corporation tax on their profits, whether or not they are distributed. With effect from 6 April 1993, UK resident shareholders are given a tax credit that is equivalent to the lower rate of income tax of 20 per cent on the dividend they receive. They are therefore deemed to have received income equal to the dividend plus the tax credit but the tax credit is deemed to offset the lower rate tax liability due on that total amount of income. This system prevents double taxation of distributed profits in the hands of both the company and the individual shareholder.

When paying a dividend, the company has to account to the Revenue for an amount equal to the tax credit, except in respect of 1993/94 when the company has to account for an amount calculated by reference to the rate of 22.5 per cent. The payment made by the company to the Revenue when making a distribution is known as advance corporation tax (ACT) and, generally, that amount can be set against the company's mainstream tax liability.

Trading/investment companies

A company is defined in the legislation as 'any body corporate or unincorporated association' but does not include a partnership or local authority. There are two main types of company covered by the tax legislation:

- Trading companies
- Investment companies.

The distinction is important because there are differences in the way these companies are taxed. The concept of 'trade' involves a more active and dynamic engagement than an investment activity. The legislation does not give a useful definition of trade and the Courts have been reluctant to provide a universal definition either. Thus the question of whether or not there is a trade must be decided on the facts of each case.

Elements of a trading company's tax computation

A trading company's tax computation details all the income and gains chargeable to taxation under the various taxation schedules (as outlined in the introduction). The format of a typical tax computation may be as follows.

XYZ Limited
Corporation Tax Computation
Year ended 31 March 1994

	£'000
Schedule A – rental income	X
Schedule D Case I – adjusted trading profit	X
Schedule D Case III – Interest income	X
Schedule D Case V – Overseas dividends	X
Schedule D Case VI	X
TOTAL INCOME	X
Chargeable gains	X
TOTAL PROFITS	X
LESS Charges on income	(X)
PROFITS CHARGEABLE TO CORPORATION TAX	X
Corporation Tax thereon	X
LESS Double tax relief	(X)
LESS Advance Corporation Tax	(X)
Corporation Tax payable	X

The calculation of the Schedule D Case I taxable profits would normally be calculated on a supporting schedule and might appear as follows:

XYZ Limited
Year ended 31 March 1994
Schedule D Case I Adjustment of Profit

	£'000	£'000
Profit before tax per accounts		X
Add: Depreciation	X	
Disallowable entertaining	X	
Bad debt provision – increase	X	
Charges on income	X	
Expensive leased car rental disallowance	X	
		X
Less: Sch D III untaxed UK interest	X	
Profit on sale of fixed assets	X	
Capital allowances	X	(X)
Schedule D Case I profit		X

Profits chargeable to tax
For trading companies, the income from all sources is chargeable to corporation tax and is arrived at by aggregating net trading income (Schedule D Case I) with taxable income from other sources – for example, property rentals, dividends from non-UK resident companies and chargeable gains. Charges on income are then deducted to give the net amount on which corporation tax is payable.

Trading income
Net trading income taxable under Schedule D Case I is calculated by adjusting the accounting profit (based on the ordinary principles of sound commercial accounting) for:

- Non-deductible expenses (add back)
- Income not taxable under the provisions of Schedule D Case I (subtract)
- Depreciation charged in the accounts (substitute capital allowances).

Non-deductible expenses
Since it is the net income from a trade that is taxable and not the gross receipts, there is a basic presumption that trading expenses are deductible for tax purposes. Therefore, in the absence of any express prohibition, expenses will be deductible.

For expenses to be deductible in computing trading profits, they must be 'wholly and exclusively laid out for the purposes of the trade'. Wholly and exclusively is not defined in the legislation, but case law indicates that expenditure which lacks singularity of purpose is not tax deductible. In addition, other items that are not allowable in computing trading profit include:

- Expenditure of a capital nature: The distinction between capital and revenue expenditure is not defined in the legislation but case law indicates that expenditure that gives rise to an enduring benefit to the trade is capital – for example, improvements to business premises, legal costs connected with the acquisition of capital assets, company formation expense, and expenses of raising capital other than loan capital fulfilling certain conditions
- Business entertainment (excluding staff entertainment)
- Depreciation of fixed assets: Capital allowances may be given instead (see below)
- Bad or doubtful debt provisions (unless they are made in respect of specific debts) and any other general provisions included within the accounts. A deduction may only be obtained for specific provisions – that is, those calculated accurately with reference to known individual amounts that relate to the period for which the computation is being prepared. General provisions – for example, estimated amounts – are not allowable
- Loan interest (other than UK bank interest and 'short interest') and patent royalties (such interest and royalties may be deductible as charges on income – see below)
- Foreign taxes relieved by way of tax credit (see section on taxation of foreign income)
- A proportion of the rental payable on leased cars whose original market value exceeds £12,000.

Capital allowances

Depreciation charged in the accounts to amortise capital assets is not tax deductible. Instead, expenditure on certain kinds of assets attracts capital allowances which are treated as a deduction from taxable trading income. The more common classes of expenditure for which capital allowances are available include:

- Industrial buildings used for the purposes of a manufacturing or similar trade (allowances: 4 per cent per annum straight line basis except that a 20 per cent initial allowance applies to expenditure during the year ending 31 October 1993)
- Plant and machinery, including commercial vehicles (allowances: 25 per cent per annum on the reducing balance basis, except that a 40 per cent first year allowance applies for expenditure incurred during the year ending 31 October 1993)

- Motor cars, original market value less than, currently, £12,000 (allowances: 25 per cent per annum on the reducing balance basis)
- Motor cars, original market value greater than, currently, £12,000 (allowances: 25 per cent per annum on the reducing balance basis, subject to a maximum of £3,000 per annum)
- Know-how and patents – as for plant and machinery

Allowances are available from the date when expenditure is incurred (except on industrial buildings, where allowances are available from the date the building is brought into use). All or part of the allowances may be disclaimed, which may be beneficial to optimise the tax position, in certain circumstances.

There are a number of specific assets for which special rules may apply. These include short life plant and machinery (assets whose useful life is less than 5 years), assets used to carry out scientific research, buildings in Enterprise Zones, assets used in the extraction of oil and minerals, hotels and second hand buildings.

Income not taxable under the provisions of Schedule D Case I
This includes income that is taxable under the provisions of another case (for example, UK bank deposit interest, which is taxed under Schedule D Case III, and foreign income, which is taxable under Schedule D Case V) and income that is not taxable in the hands of a UK trading company.

Trading losses
Should the adjustment of the accounts profit (or loss) under Schedule D Case I give rise to a trading loss for tax purposes, then there are a number of ways in which the trading loss may be utilised, including:

- Set off against the company's income and gains from other sources liable to corporation tax in the same accounting period
- Carry back and set off against total profits of the three years preceding the accounting period in which the loss was incurred, relieving the latest profits first (this applies for accounting periods ended after 31 March 1991)
- Surrendered by way of group relief to other group companies
- Losses unrelieved above may be carried forward indefinitely, to be set off against future trading profits from the same trade.

Chargeable gains
Chargeable gains or losses arise on the disposal of capital assets that are held by companies. Broadly, on disposal of the asset, the increase in value from the purchase date (subject to certain rules) to the date of disposal is charged to corporation tax.

For individuals, the gain on disposal is calculated in the same manner as for companies but is known as a capital gain and is subject to capital gains tax.

Prior to the introduction of capital gains tax in 1965, a company could dispose of non trading assets at a profit without giving rise to a tax liability. Between 1965 and 1982, no allowance was made for the effect of inflation and the whole of any chargeable gain was subject to tax rather than just the real gain. This problem was addressed over a period of time from 1982, and largely solved in the Finance Act, 1988, by the introduction of rebasing to 31 March 1982.

Rebasing means that the market value of an asset held at 31 March 1982 replaces the actual cost of the asset for the purposes of the chargeable gains calculation. Inflation since March 1982 is taken into account by an indexation allowance, which is based on the movement in the retail price index since March 1982 or the date of acquisition, if later.

Chargeable gains (less allowable capital losses) made by companies are included within profits chargeable to corporation tax.

The chargeable gain is calculated by deducting the base cost of the asset, and an indexation allowance, from disposal proceeds. A calculation of chargeable gains/losses in relation to disposals after 6 April 1988 might appear as follows:

	£
Gross proceeds of disposal	X
Less costs of disposal	(X)
Net proceeds	X
Less: cost of asset (or 31 March 1982 market value, if higher, and asset acquired prior to that date)	(X)
	X
Less: Indexation allowance	(X)
Chargeable gain/allowable loss	X

The main relief available for chargeable gains realised on assets used in a trade is 'Rollover' relief. This relief is available where qualifying business assets are sold and replaced with other qualifying assets. The tax on the gain can be deferred, broadly, until the disposal of the replacement asset.

If the capital gains calculation gives rise to a capital loss on the disposal of the asset, these losses may be offset against chargeable gains arising to the company in the same period. Any excess losses remaining can then be carried forward for offset against future chargeable gains arising in the same company. They cannot be carried back against gains of an earlier accounting period, as is the case with trading losses.

Charges on income

Charges on income are recurring annual payments that are not deductible in computing trading profits but instead, provided certain conditions are met, are deductible from total profits from all sources (including capital gains).

The main types of charges on income are:

- Annual interest (generally interest on loans of more than one year)
- Patent royalties
- Payments under a deed of covenant.

These must actually be paid during the accounting period in order to rank for tax relief. In most circumstances, income tax should be deducted from the payment when made and the tax paid over to the Inland Revenue. The recipient of the income is then deemed to have suffered tax at the basic rate on their income.

Tax rates

Corporation tax is currently charged at 33 per cent for the financial year 1993. For companies whose profits (including chargeable gains and franked investment income) do not exceed certain limits (presently £250,000), the small companies rate of 25 per cent may apply. Where total profits are above £250,000 and less than £1,250,000, there is a marginal relief, to reduce the overall rate of tax to between 25 per cent and 33 per cent.

The limits are reduced if the company has one or more active associated companies (including non-resident companies) at any time during the accounting period in question.

Advance Corporation Tax

When a UK resident company pays a dividend, it must pay Advance Corporation Tax (ACT) to the Revenue. ACT is charged at a prescribed rate. For 1993/94, the rate is 22.5/77.5ths of the cash amount of the dividend paid to the shareholders and, for 1994/5, it will be 20/80ths. It is not a deduction from the dividend but, instead, an additional amount that the company must pay at the time a dividend payment is made. As the name implies, it is an advance payment of the company's liability to corporation tax and is recoverable against the tax on the profits of the accounting period in which the dividend is paid, subject to certain limits.

A tax credit (normally equivalent to the amount of ACT paid by the company, although not the case for 1993/94) attaches to the dividend received by the shareholder, and is deemed to cover the tax liability of a shareholder who is subject to tax at the basic rate on the dividend.

Dividends by one UK resident company received from another UK resident company are exempt from corporation tax. The tax credit attached to these dividends through the tax credit mechanism can be set against any ACT that the company has to account for when it pays a dividend itself. This is done through a system of quarterly accounting returns.

Any ACT in excess of the maximum set off available against the total corporation tax liability of that period is known as surplus ACT and can either be carried back for up to six years or be carried forward for set off against the total tax liabilities of future years, or surrendered to the company's subsidiaries. Surplus ACT that is not capable of being recovered in the foreseeable future is normally written off in a company's accounts, and is therefore shown as an additional tax charge.

Groups and consortia

A group of companies for tax purposes normally means two or more UK resident companies where one owns beneficially, whether directly or indirectly, more than 50 per cent of the issued ordinary share capital of the other (that is, a 51 per cent group). For certain purposes, different percentage shareholdings are required (for example, a 75 per cent group).

Consolidation

Under UK tax law, every company is treated as an independent taxable entity. There is no general provision for consolidated group tax treatment – for example, filing of consolidated tax returns – as there is in some other countries.

Groups and consortia are afforded special tax treatment to try to ensure that separate companies in a group are not disadvantaged in comparison with a company that carries on a number of activities as separate divisions.

Reliefs for groups of companies

The reliefs available to a 75 per cent group include:

- Trading losses, excess charges on income, and certain other tax losses can be surrendered by one group company to another
- Capital assets can generally be transferred between group members without liability to tax on capital gains
- Surrender of ACT from a parent to its subsidiaries.

An additional relief available to 51 per cent groups is that dividends and charges on income can be paid under a formal election ('group income election') between group members, without accounting for ACT and income tax respectively.

Certain of the above reliefs are also available, in a more restricted form, to members of a consortium. A UK trading company is part of a consortium, if at least 75 per cent of the ordinary share capital is held by other UK resident companies of which none individually owns less than 5 per cent. The companies that together hold the share capital of the trading company are known as consortium members.

Investment companies

Investment companies may be either investment dealing companies, which are treated as trading companies and taxed under Schedule D Case I, or investment holding companies, whose income (excluding dividends from UK resident companies) is taxed as investment income. Management expenses and charges on income are deductible in computing taxable profits of an investment holding company.

Approved investment trusts, which are quoted UK resident investment holding companies satisfying certain stringent conditions, are exempt from tax on capital gains, as are unit trusts.

Close companies

A 'close company' is a UK resident company that, broadly, is controlled by five or fewer persons or by shareholder/directors – these persons are known as participators. There is exemption for certain companies, that, although closely controlled, have a minimum 35 per cent public shareholding and are quoted on a recognised stock exchange.

Prior to the 1989 Finance Act, undistributed income of close trading companies could be apportioned to shareholders who would then be liable to tax on the deemed income unless the company paid a minimum level of dividend. Now the provisions apply only to close investment holding companies – in other words, closely held passive investment companies. The object of this is to prevent individuals using companies to accumulate income that will be taxed at the lower Corporation Tax rate of 33% rather than the higher income tax rate of 40 per cent.

Benefits in kind provided for participators of any close company are deemed to be distributions and hence the recipients are taxed as if they received a dividend and ACT must be accounted for by the company.

If a close company makes a loan to an individual who is a participator, the company is required to account to the Revenue for an amount equal to the ACT that would be payable if its loan was a dividend; this ACT is recoverable when the loan is repaid.

Taxation of sole traders and partnerships

Trading income arising to sole traders or partnerships is assessed on the individuals concerned and hence is chargeable to income tax rather than corporation tax. Income tax is currently chargeable at the basic rate of 25 per cent, apart from the first £2,500 of taxable income which is taxed at 20 per cent. On taxable income over £23,700, the rate of income tax is currently 40 per cent.

Sole traders

Sole traders are subject to income tax on the profits of their business under the provisions of Schedule D Case I (trades) or Case II (professions). The accounting profits are adjusted to arrive at profits chargeable to tax in the same way as companies' profits are adjusted for corporation tax purposes.

The taxable income for an income tax year of assessment of the business profits of a sole trader is calculated, except in the opening and closing years of the business, by reference to the income of the accounting period that ended in the previous tax year.

Unlike companies, which are taxed for an accounting period, individuals are taxed for an income tax year. In normal circumstances, when the business is ongoing, the profits chargeable to tax for any income tax year will be based on the profits arising in the accounting period of the sole trader ending in the previous income tax year.

In the opening and closing years, an election may be made by the taxpayer or the Inspector of Taxes respectively, that the profits chargeable to tax will be based on actual figures rather than on the prior year basis as described above.

Partnerships

A partnership is not, in law, a legal entity separate from its individual members (except in Scotland). The income tax liability under Schedule D Cases I or II for a partnership is computed in a similar manner as for a sole trader.

Partnerships are also normally taxed on a prior year basis – that is, by reference to the accounting period ending in the previous income tax year. This rule can be overridden in the case of a change in the partnership (that is, if any of the individuals change) or in the opening and closing years.

The income tax liability of a partnership of individuals is computed jointly and a single assessment is raised on the partnership. The adjusted profits are allocated between the partners based on their profit sharing ratios and each partner's liability to tax on their share of partnership profits is calculated (after taking into account other personal income and reliefs) and the aggregate of the partners' liabilities is assessed on the partnership as a single assessment.

The opening and closing year rules are also similar to those of sole traders.

Taxation of international businesses

Many businesses are conducted on an international scale, either through a multinational group of companies or by means of a UK based company exporting to numerous other countries or operating in these other counties via branches.

There is an important distinction between a UK company 'trading with' (that is, exporting to) and 'trading in' (that is, selling via a local branch/permanent establishment) an overseas country.

A UK company trading with an overseas country would not normally pay local tax on profits generated from those sales, while a company trading in such a country is likely to pay local tax on its branch profits. Similarly, in the UK, overseas companies that are trading in the UK will be subject to corporation tax on the profits so arising but companies only trading with the UK will not be subject to corporation tax.

A potential problem is double taxation, in that profits arising may be taxed in more than one jurisdiction, as a result of the fact that UK resident companies are taxed on their world-wide profits. The UK has special rules and double tax treaties with a number of countries in an attempt to prevent double taxation.

Taxation of foreign income

Income arising from overseas to UK resident traders is taxed under Schedule D Cases IV and V, being income from securities outside the UK and income from foreign possessions respectively. Tax is chargeable on the amount of income arising, whether or not this is remitted to the UK (although there is some relief where the income is unremittable). Profits from a trade carried on partly in the UK and partly overseas are taxed under Schedule D Case I.

Double tax relief is available for most foreign tax suffered. Such relief is given as a credit to the UK resident, and is limited to the UK tax attributable to such foreign income or gains on a source by source basis. Any foreign tax credits in excess of the UK tax on that income are not available for double tax relief and are permanently lost. In some cases, it may be preferable to claim foreign tax paid as an expense rather than claim credit relief – for example, when there are no net profits chargeable to corporation tax and the credit relief would otherwise be permanently lost.

Subject to the special legislation dealing with controlled foreign companies (see below), the profits of non UK resident subsidiaries (where they do not arise in the UK) are not subject to UK tax until they are distributed as dividends to UK residents.

The controlled foreign company ('CFC') legislation is aimed at preventing tax avoidance through tax haven operations and is designed to charge UK companies to tax on untaxed or lightly taxed profits of particular overseas subsidiaries. A foreign company may fall within the legislation, if it is not UK resident but is controlled by UK residents, and is subject to a lower level of taxation in its country of residence. There are a number of exceptions to prevent companies falling within this legislation to cover situations where:

- The overseas company pursues an acceptable distribution policy
- The overseas company carries on exempt activities (for example, commercial trading)
- Chargeable profits of the CFC are less than £20,000 for the year
- The motive for the CFC's existence is not the reduction of UK liability to tax.

Taxation of foreign companies

Subject to the provisions of a double taxation treaty, a non resident company carrying on a trade in the United Kingdom through a branch or agency is chargeable to UK tax on the following:

- Any trading income arising directly or indirectly from the branch or agency
- Any income from property or rights used by or held by the branch or agency
- Capital gains arising on the disposal of assets situated in the UK
- Unrealised capital gains on assets situated in the UK, that are removed from the UK.

The profits of the branch chargeable to corporation tax under Schedule D Case I are calculated in a similar way to those for UK resident companies. However, there are two main differences in the tax treatment of foreign companies:

- Small companies rate relief is not available, which means that the full corporation tax rate is chargeable even on profits below £250,000
- ACT is not payable in relation to dividends paid by the foreign company.

Transfer pricing

Groups of companies have the opportunity to adjust prices for transactions between members of the group to increase profits in one company and reduce profits in another. This is termed 'transfer pricing' and, clearly, particularly between group companies in different countries, this can be exploited to achieve certain tax advantages. To counter such potential tax avoidance, the Inland Revenue has the power to, in effect, calculate taxable profits or losses arising on transactions between a UK resident company and its non UK resident affiliates as if the transaction had been carried out on arm's length terms. This not only applies to sales of trading stock but also to interest, royalties, management charges etc. Where such an adjustment is made in connection with a transaction carried out with an overseas affiliate resident in a country with which the United Kingdom has a double tax treaty, the treaty may contain a provision requiring a corresponding adjustment in the other country, so that the taxable profits of the overseas affiliates are adjusted accordingly.

Double tax treaties

The United Kingdom has a large network of double tax treaties, under which double taxation is prevented either by exempting the income or gains from taxation in one of the territories, or by granting a tax credit in the other for tax payable in the territory in which the income or gain arose.

In addition, the double tax treaties often provide for a reduced rate of withholding tax on interest, dividends, or royalties or any payment between the two territories. This withholding tax suffered is also available for double tax relief, as described above.

Double tax treaties seek to clarify in which country income should be charged to tax. For companies, many treaties provide that the trading profits will be taxable in a country if there is deemed to be a 'permanent establishment' in that country. A permanent establishment is defined in each treaty and the meaning varies but, generally, it means a fixed place of business through which the trade is wholly or partly carried on. This definition results in the taxation of a UK trading branch of an overseas company in the UK.

Value Added Tax

VAT is charged on the supply of goods and services in the United Kingdom made by a taxable person in the course or furtherance of any business, unless that supply is an exempt supply (or is zero rated).

Basic principles

VAT is a tax on consumer expenditure and, in theory, should not fall on business activities. This is achieved by the input/output system. Input tax is payable on goods or services purchased and output tax is charged on sales made to other businesses or the final customer. The net difference between input and output tax is accounted for by the trader to Customs and Excise on a quarterly basis.

Taxable supplies

The provision of goods or services in the UK by a taxable person is known as a supply for VAT purposes. Such supplies are either exempt from VAT or chargeable at the standard rate or zero rated.

Most exempt supplies are services, the main ones being insurance and banking services, education, certain health services and sales and leases of second-hand buildings. Although the provision of such exempt supplies does not require output tax to be charged thereon, no input tax may be deducted in respect of these supplies, and hence businesses making such supplies will incur a real cost in the form of non-deductible input tax. If the business makes only exempt supplies, there may be a partially offsetting benefit in that it does not need to involve itself with the administration of the VAT system.

Some input tax is always non-deductible to any business. Examples include VAT on motor cars and business entertaining expenditure.

Zero rated supplies are used extensively in the UK and relate to exports and necessities such as domestic food and water, fuel and power, children's clothing, passenger transport, books and newspapers. Unlike the position with regard to exempt supplies, input tax related to zero rated outputs is recoverable by the trader.

All supplies not falling within the above categories are standard rated.

VAT is charged on the supply of goods and services in the United Kingdom. In addition, VAT is charged on imports at the same rate as domestic production, but is similarly deductible as input tax to a trader.

1993

With effect from 1 January 1993, VAT is no longer payable on imports of goods from other member states of the EC, though VAT liability remains in force in respect of imports from outside the EC.

Further changes also came into effect on the same day in respect of exports. Although the general zero rating for exports of goods to destinations outside the EC was retained, it is now necessary to know (and to show on the sales invoice) the VAT registration number of the customer before any sale to destinations within the EC may be zero rated. There are special rules in relation to sale of private motor cars, boats and aircraft (they are taxed in the country of registration) and certain mail order and direct selling operations.

Tax rates

For taxable supplies, there are at present two VAT rates in use in the UK:

- Standard rate (17.5 per cent)
- Zero rate.

These rates apply to both goods and services. It is proposed that for the year ending 31 March 1995, a VAT rate of eight per cent will be applied to domestic fuel and power (thereafter, the standard rate will apply).

Other indirect taxes

Customs and Excise duties

Customs duties are chargeable on goods brought into the United Kingdom from outside the EC.

Excise duties are chargeable on certain items – for example, alcoholic drinks, tobacco products, certain forms of betting and gaming, hydrocarbon oil etc. Relief from duty may be available, in certain circumstances, on goods that are exported from the United Kingdom or are of a particular description.

Stamp Duty

Stamp duty is levied on written documents relating to certain transactions. It is the document itself, and not the transaction, which makes stamp duty payable.

There have been a number of changes to the stamp duty system in recent years and a number of duties abolished. The most important duties remaining are the duties on sales and leases of property and land. Stamp duties on shares and other securities will possibly be abolished from April 1994, along with stamp duty reserve tax which presently applies to certain transactions in securities.

If there is a requirement for a document to be stamped and it is not in fact stamped, it is inadmissible as evidence in a UK Court.

Stamp duty is payable, in theory, when the document is executed. In practice, the Revenue allows a period of grace of 30 days. It is possible to have a document stamped subsequently but there are penalties for late stamping.

Uniform Business Rates

This is a tax based on the annual rental value of non domestic properties, in order to finance local government expenditure.

Rates are normally payable by the occupiers. They are calculated by reference to the rateable value of the property and a multiplier, which is set for England with separate figures for Wales and Scotland. Rates are collected by the charging authority and the proceeds paid to central government for redistribution on a per capita basis.

This system was adopted on 1 April 1990 and certain transitional rules apply in order to protect existing ratepayers from otherwise unacceptable increases arising from the introduction of the uniform business rates.

Personal financial and tax planning

Personal financial planning and tax planning are interdependent. An investment strategy cannot be developed without consideration of the taxation implications, and vice versa.

Furthermore, the achievement of a successful personal financial strategy involves co-ordinated advice on all of the areas that impact upon an individual's present position and the achievement of his financial aspirations. These include:

- Investments
- Legal issues
- Pensions
- Insurance
- Taxation implications.

Personal financial planning

Increasingly, individuals use qualified financial planners to plan and direct their personal financial strategy. As a starting point, the planner will determine the total resources of the client, together with actual or anticipated assets and liabilities. He will also determine his client's present and future financial needs, aspirations and goals and consider how best to achieve those aims, bearing in mind the following:

- The client's attitude to risk
- The purpose of the investment
- The time frame for the achievement of aims and objectives.

Then, the planner can construct a financial plan and, with the agreement of his client, can implement it. Naturally, the plan is not 'set in stone' and the planner will need to try to anticipate the changes in the financial and taxation circumstances of his client.

Investment strategy

The planner's aim is to assist the client in achieving his objectives in the most tax efficient and low risk manner available. This involves the development of an investment and planning strategy that matches the client's needs and aspirations, which may include:

Client needs	**Investment match example**
Protection of assets from the effects of inflation	Index-Linked Government stocks Index-Linked National Saving certificates
Capital growth and income	Government stocks (Gilts) Shares Collective investment schemes Personal equity plans (PEPs)
Capital growth, no income	Zero dividend preference shares Business Expansion Schemes (BES) Enterprise Zones (EZ)
Income	Bank/building society accounts Tax Exempt Special Savings Accounts (TESSAs)
Providing for retirement	Additional Voluntary Contributions (AVCs)
Family protection	Family Income Bond (FIB) Permanent Health Insurance (PHI)
Family provision	Capital Investment Strategy Endowment policies Term assurance

Financial planners are regularly called upon to advise on the following key topics:

- Tax shelters
- Pensions
- Family protection and provision
- Independent taxation
- Capital Gains Tax planning
- Inheritance Tax planning.

Tax shelters

There are, broadly, three types of tax shelter:

- Those that give tax relief up front when purchasing an investment – Business Expansion Schemes and Enterprise Zone investments, and pensions
- Those that give freedom from taxation on income and gains rolled up within the investment itself – Personal Equity Plans (PEPs) and Tax Exempt Special Savings Accounts (TESSAs), and again pensions
- Those that have no tax liability arising upon encashment – pensions.

There is a broad range of insurance products that not only provide life cover, but also a means of saving. For example, a traditional endowment policy is useful for building up a tax free lump sum and, in some cases, proceeds can be withdrawn free of all taxes after seven and a half years.

Longer term policies are free of tax after three quarters of the term or ten years, whichever is earlier. There is a potential charge to higher rate tax on the surrender of the policy within the shorter of ten years or three quarters of the policy paying term. No charges to CGT should arise on payment of the policy proceeds.

A further example is the Unit Linked Single Premium (Investment) Bond which is a non-qualifying life assurance policy in which lump sums are invested. There is minimal life cover. There is no income tax charge on withdrawals from the bond to basic rate taxpayers. Higher rate taxpayers can avoid or defer the charge in certain circumstances. There is normally no CGT liability on the policy proceeds in the hands of the investor.

Business Expansion Scheme

The purpose of the Business Expansion Scheme (BES) has been to encourage investment in unlimited companies, as an indirect means of job creation. Individuals who invest in 'qualifying companies' (that is, companies approved under the Scheme by the Inland Revenue) may write off the cost of their investment against their income for tax purposes in the year in which it is made. Income and capital gains arising on the investment are tax free, provided the investment is held for at least five years. Any tax relief given may be clawed back, if the investment is sold before the end of the five year period.

The intention of the scheme was that investors would use it to mitigate the risks of investing in high risk businesses, particularly start ups. However, even with the tax incentives offered, investors prefer asset backing to high risk exposure and the scheme has been repeatedly amended in order to outlaw abuses.

For the most part, BES opportunities presently available are provided by companies investing in housing let under assured tenancy arrangements. The most attractive are those that offer an assured 'exit' for investors at the end of their minimum investment period (five years). These particular BES offer projected returns of around 16 per cent per annum to a 40 per cent taxpayer.

During 1993/94, it is possible to invest up to £40,000 in a BES and obtain tax relief up front at the higher marginal rate. Thus, to a 40 per cent taxpayer, the true cost of the maximum investment is £24,000. However, the BES will be abolished at the end of December 1993.

Enterprise Zones

EZ are located throughout Britain, in places as far apart as Tayside and Kent. Most are in areas needing economic regeneration.

The capital cost of constructing commercial property located in an EZ attracts 100 per cent tax relief (excluding the land element). A proportion of the investment can be funded with borrowed money, on which tax relief may be available. Thus, if the rental income can service the borrowing, the project can become (largely) self-financing.

The large investor may consider purchasing a single building, either by himself or with a group of other investors. For the smaller investor, there is the option of collective investment schemes where funds are pooled for the purchase of property or a series of properties.

Provided certain conditions are met, an individual may claim tax relief in full in either the tax year of purchase or the following tax year; or part of it in the year of purchase or following year and the remainder over a period of four years.

If the building is sold within 25 years, the tax relief may be clawed back at the individual's tax rate at the time.

Personal Equity Plans

Personal Equity Plans (PEPs) allow an investor to invest up to £6,000 (1993/94) each year in a plan with the following features:

- The income and capital gains can be rolled-up free from tax
- The plan can be closed and the investments withdrawn at any time without a charge to tax arising.

The plan must be managed by a plan manager and the investment must be in quoted UK equities, or collective investment schemes (that is, unit or investment trusts) that meet certain requirements.

From 1 January 1992, an individual may invest up to £3,000 in a single company PEP (in addition to the £6,000 general PEP allowance) invested in shares of a single quoted UK company. Furthermore, it is possible for shares held under an employee-wide share scheme to be transferred straight into this type of PEP without a charge to capital gains tax arising on the disposal.

Tax Exempt Special Savings Accounts

Banks and building societies have been operating TESSAs since April 1991. Many are offering very attractive rates of tax free interest or bonuses, quoted over a five year minimum investment period.

The maximum investment is £9,000, spread over the five year period, with a maximum of £3,000 being invested in the first year, £1,800 in years two, three and four and £600 in year five.

Deposits may not be withdrawn until the fifth anniversary of the opening of the TESSA. If withdrawn sooner, the tax exempt status is lost. Interest or bonuses may be withdrawn, although an amount equal to income tax at the basic rate will be retained in the account.

Pensions

Adequate provision for retirement forms the core of a personal financial and tax planning strategy. Whether employed or self-employed, individuals have a much greater freedom now than previously to organise their pensions.

Pensions may be either company sponsored schemes or personal pensions arrangements.

Company sponsored schemes

For most employee members of a company pension scheme, the Inland Revenue approves pension entitlement as a fraction not exceeding two thirds of remuneration, as defined.

For employees who joined their present pension scheme after 31 March 1989 (in some cases, 13 March 1989), the remuneration to which the two thirds fraction is applied is capped at £75,000 for 1993/94.

One way of enhancing pension benefits is to pay Additional Voluntary Contributions (AVCs) to the company scheme, within the limit of 15 per cent of salary (including bonuses and taxable benefits in kind). AVCs can be paid either to the employer's scheme or to another scheme of the employee's own choice (free standing AVCs).

Bonuses may be paid into the scheme to boost the pension benefits (bonus sacrifice). It may also be possible to forego a prospective right to future remuneration and for the company to contribute this to a pension plan or scheme (salary sacrifice).

At retirement, part of the fund accumulated may be used to provide a lump sum. This lump sum pension commutation is tax free but the pension received in retirement from the balance of the fund is still subject to income tax. There is thus good reason to take the maximum possible lump sum, which is limited by law to one and a half times remuneration.

Personal pensions

Personal Pension Plans (PPP) were introduced with effect from 1 July 1988. Unlike company sponsored (or occupational) pension schemes, a PPP can be retained by an individual notwithstanding changes in his employment. It is, therefore, possible to transfer accrued benefits from one employment to another. Of course, the transfer of benefits can also take place from one occupational scheme to another, although with by no means the same degree of flexibility – usually, transfers involve a significant loss of benefits, which can inhibit job mobility.

Under a PPP, an employee makes his own contributions to his pensions provider. Where his employer makes additional contributions to an employee's PPP, these do not constitute 'earnings' for tax or National Insurance purposes. This is very attractive to the higher rate taxpayer, who would otherwise have to earn a much higher sum before tax in order to make the same contribution to his personal pension.

PPPs replaced Retirement Annuity Policies (RAPs) on 1 July 1988. RAPs effected before 1 July 1988 can be continued (subject to the policy arrangements) or can be switched to a PPP.

In the case of PPPs, or pre 1 July 1988 RAPs, the self-employed and those in non-pensionable employment may claim tax relief for premiums paid. In each case, the maximum allowable contributions are based on a percentage of the individual's 'Net Relevant Earnings'. For those over 35, the percentages are higher for PPPs than for RAPs. Counterbalancing this, for PPPs there is a ceiling on total contributions based on the 'earnings cap' (currently, £75,000).

Contributions may be carried back one year (or exceptionally, two years) for tax purposes, whereas unused relief may be brought forward from the previous six years if relief for the tax year of claim has been fully utilised.

Further pensions flexibility was introduced as a result of the 1988 changes. Upon the attainment of selected retirement age, the individual is not bound to keep his pension fund with the chosen insurance company. By using the open market option to transfer the pension fund to another insurance company with better annuity rates, it may be possible to improve pension benefits considerably. However, this may affect adversely the amount of tax free cash available.

Family protection and provision

Any personal financial and tax plan must address the need for the main breadwinner to protect dependants from the financial effects of a disruption to the family's income, either as a result of death or permanent disability. Provision must also be made for future needs — for example, the education of children.

Family protection

Most employees are covered by death in service insurance provided by their employer, often as part of an employee pension scheme. The insurance will provide a multiple of the employee's salary as a lump sum to a nominated beneficiary upon death occurring while in service. A widow's (or, more rarely, a widower's) pension may also be payable when the widow (widower) reaches retirement age.

Although the lump sum can cushion the blow in the short term, it will often be insufficient to purchase the necessary income requirement to maintain the survivors, particularly where a young family is involved.

If the family home is being paid for with an endowment mortgage, the related endowment policy will pay off the outstanding mortgage but, again, the income requirements of the young family left without the main source of income may remain unmet.

Alternatively, the breadwinner may be unable to work by reasons of disability, as a result of which the family's standard of living could fall considerably. This fall could be aggravated further by the medical costs associated with such illness.

To protect against the financial effects of an untimely death, a Family Income Benefit (FIB) policy can be effected. Broadly, this provides annual tax free income for dependants should death occur during a specified term from the date of issue of the policy.

To avoid the financial constraints arising from permanent disability, Permanent Health Insurance (PHI) cover can be effected. This would provide a weekly or monthly income until retirement age, in the event of the person insured becoming disabled and unable to work.

Family provision

The other leg of financial and tax planning, insofar as it impacts upon the family, is family provision. Although this can take many forms, the prime example is school fees provision.

In the UK, more than 500,000 children are currently being educated at approximately 2,500 private schools. In each of the past ten years, the average cost of educating a child privately has outpaced the rise in the Retail Prices Index (RPI). The conventional way of ensuring adequate provision for school fees is to schedule fees and their due dates, in order to establish the total liability for each of the years concerned. It is then, as with all financial and tax planning tasks, a matter of matching assets to liabilities. Thus, the assets structure will be determined by the liabilities.

Generally, the approach should be:

- Plan as early as possible
- Plan with maximum flexibility
- Do not restrict planning to packaged products (that is, do not overlook savings by PEPs and TESSAs)
- See whether grandparents can assist
- Where possible avoid borrowing.

Tax planning

Personal financial and tax planning should be considered concurrently. There are numerous planning opportunities provided by current taxation legislation. So far as income tax is concerned, one of the most important recent changes has been that relating to the taxation of married couples.

Independent taxation

Historically, a married man was responsible in law for making returns of his income, which was deemed to include any income his wife earned. Allowances and reliefs were allocated by the tax authorities against the husband's income and there were limited opportunities to transfer allowances between spouses. In addition, while two single people each received the single person's personal allowance, a married woman received no allowance in her own name.

From 6 April 1990, husbands and wives each have been entitled to their respective income tax and Capital Gains Tax reliefs and allowances. A married woman now has her own reliefs and allowances available to be set against her own income and any capital gains. Furthermore, she also has her own basic rate tax band, within which income is taxed at 20 per cent on the first £2,000 of taxable income above her personal allowance and at 25 per cent thereafter, up to £23,700.

Additionally, transfers of assets between husband and wife are usually completely free of Capital Gains Tax and, where both spouses are domiciled or non-domiciled in the UK, Inheritance Tax.

Clearly, as well as recognising the independence of working wives, the new regime gives couples ample scope for tax planning. The aim of such planning is to move income out of the hands of the spouse paying tax at the higher marginal rate to the spouse whose income is taxable at the lower rates, or who does not pay tax at all.

For example, a husband could consider employing his wife in a family business or partnership. If he pays her a salary equivalent to her personal allowance plus the lower tax bands, the couple's net take home pay will be higher than if he increased his salary, taxable at the higher rate, by the same amount. Alternatively, he could give her assets producing income or capital gains to utilise her personal allowance and lower rate bands. Having said this, it is important to ensure that such employments and gifts are genuine and are not merely paper transactions for the purposes of tax avoidance. The Inland Revenue will look beyond form to substance.

Children's Personal Allowances

Another related area of income tax planning is the maximising of Personal Allowances. For example, a child has its own Personal Allowance (presently £3,445) and annual CGT exemption (currently £5,800). Income and capital up to these limits respectively are not taxable although, where the child's own parents provide funds that generate income, the income is treated as the income of the parents (subject to a *de minimis* exemption of £100 per annum).

Deeds of covenant (effectively, a binding agreement) from grandparents to their grandchildren to provide income – perhaps to meet school fees – used to be a means of providing income to a child to use their available allowances. However, new non-charitable deeds of covenant are no longer effective. Thus an option is for grandparents to give money or investments to grandchildren so as to utilise their allowances.

Bank interest

In April 1991, a major change occurred in the way interest from banks and building society deposits was treated.

Previously, tax at the Composite Rate (deemed equivalent to the basic rate) was deducted from interest arising from the majority of cash deposits. Taxpayers grossed up the cash interest received by the amount of the tax withheld in arriving at their total taxable income and received credit for the tax paid. Thus, basic rate taxpayers paid no more tax, and higher rate taxpayers paid the difference between basic and higher rates of tax on this income. However, non-taxpayers could not reclaim the tax withheld at source.

Now, the tax deducted is basic rate tax, which is fully recoverable by the non-taxpayer. Furthermore, subject to a declaration of non-liability to tax, interest from UK bank and building society accounts can now be received gross.

Capital Gains Tax planning

Capital gains are gains arising on the disposal of chargeable assets. Most assets – property, jewellery, investments, etc – are chargeable assets, though wasting assets – those that lose value over time, like most cars, for example – are excluded.

Losses arising on disposals of chargeable assets are initially offset against gains during the year in which they arise. If there are surplus losses, they can be carried forward to future years to be set against gains not covered by the annual exemption.

An individual is exempt from Capital Gains Tax (CGT) on capital gains up to a specified amount each year (for 1993/94, £5,800). He will pay

CGT on the excess, at his marginal rate of income tax. The exemption may not be used in any year other than that to which it applies. Therefore, an important part of CGT planning is to realise sufficient gains each year to use up the annual exemption.

The annual CGT exemption is not transferable between spouses. Independent taxation of spouses (see above) offers opportunities to equalise assets between spouses. Clients will usually be advised to do this so that each spouse holds sufficient assets, which themselves have inherent gains, to ensure each annual exemption is not wasted and that any gains charged to CGT are taxed on the spouse with the lower marginal rate, if possible.

In some circumstances, it is possible to realise a gain or a loss on investments by sale and repurchase transactions (so called 'bed and breakfasting') during a Stock Exchange account period. The shares are sold at a price that ensures the gain is within the annual exemption. They are then immediately repurchased, at more or less the same price (allowing for the dealing spread). Effectively, the client has not parted with the shares, yet the gain inherent in the purchase price has been 'sheltered' by the annual exemption. In this way, an investment portfolio can be kept tax free, simply by bed and breakfasting gains within the portfolio up to the annual exemption each year.

Rebasing

For CGT purposes, the cost of assets acquired before 31 March 1982 is generally deemed to be their value at that date. However, where the original cost gives a gain on disposal and the 31 March 1982 value gives a loss, or vice versa, the disposal is deemed to be at no gain/no loss.

To avoid losing the benefit of the loss, the taxpayer may make a 'rebasing election'. This has the effect of ignoring the original cost for all assets he held on the 31 March 1982, replacing it with the 31 March 1982 value. However, the election is irrevocable and must be made within two years of the end of the tax year in which the first disposal after 5 April 1988 occurred.

Where an asset is transferred between spouses that was held by one or other at 31 March 1982, whichever one disposes of it is treated as having owned it at 31 March 1982. However, in the case of a rebasing election, the asset is treated as among those owned at 31 March 1982 by the first spouse.

Indexation

It has been deemed unfair to tax individuals on the element of the increase in the value of an asset that is due to inflation. Thus, in addition to other exemptions and allowances, for CGT purposes, an individual is also entitled to an allowance for the effects of inflation as measured by the Retail Prices Index (RPI), over the period of his ownership of the asset from acquisition or, if later, 31 March 1982. This is called Indexation Relief. The inflation-related gain is disregarded and the gain net of so called indexation is the gain upon which tax will be assessed.

Holdover Relief

Although a disposal, for CGT purposes, usually means the sale of an asset, it can also include the gifting of assets to a third party.

Where an asset is gifted in a non arm's length (that is, a non commercial) transaction, it is deemed to be sold at that date for its open market value. In certain limited circumstances, the taxpayer may elect that the gain be 'held over'.

The effect is twofold. First, it reduces the transferor's gain to nil. Second, the transferee's base cost is reduced by the same amount – in effect, he is deemed to have acquired the asset at its original cost. Therefore, when he comes later to dispose of the asset, his gain is increased by the gain held over.

Broadly, the facility to hold over the capital gains tax on lifetime gifts is limited to transfers of trading business assets (including farms) or where inheritance tax is payable on the transfer.

Retirement Relief

This relief is given where an individual over 55 (or, in the case of ill health, below the age of 55) sells a business or shares in a family trading company. The relief is an exemption of eligible gains up to £150,000, plus a reduction by 50 per cent of gains between £150,000 and £600,000.

Relief is reduced proportionately if the individual has been working in the business for less than ten years. Both husband and wife can claim retirement relief, provided that they meet the qualifying conditions.

Inheritance Tax planning

The 1986 Budget introduced significant changes to what had been known as Capital Transfer Tax, which were effective on or after that date. The tax was re-named Inheritance Tax (IHT) and the immediate charge on many lifetime gifts was effectively abolished.

Essentially, IHT provides that a transfer of value from one individual to another is a chargeable transfer unless it is an exempt transfer. A disposition is not a transfer of value if it can be shown that it was not intended to confer any gratuitous benefit upon the recipient and that it was an arm's length transaction between unconnected persons.

The rate of IHT is 40 per cent.

Exempt transfers

Exempt transfers include:

- £3,000 per donor per annum

- £250 per donee
- Normal expenditure out of income
- Gifts in consideration of marriage (£5,000 per parent, £2,500 by certain other relatives)
- Gifts to charities

Potentially exempt transfers

Certain lifetime gifts are potentially exempt and become exempt from IHT, provided that the donor survives at least seven years from the date of the gift and that the gift is of a certain class:

- Gifts to another individual or to an 'interest in possession' trust
- Gifts to a qualifying 'accumulation and maintenance' trust
- Gifts into trust for disabled people.

If the donor dies within seven years of the gift, the tax is subject to tapering relief, which takes the form of reducing the percentage of tax payable depending upon when the gift is made. Thus, until seven years has elapsed, the transfer is known as a Potentially Exempt Transfer.

However, it is important that the gift is made without the donor reserving any kind of benefit in the gifted property. If there is reservation of benefit, the gifted asset will form part of the donor's estate upon death and thus be fully subject to IHT. If an individual wishes to make gifts but does not wish to make outright transfers, he should consider using a trust. In this way, he can limit the beneficiaries' access to the property or income, whilst still reducing his overall IHT liability.

Chargeable Lifetime Transfers

In practice, a chargeable transfer in lifetime (as opposed to one potentially exempt) will be to a discretionary trust.

Lifetime transfers are charged at half the rate applicable at death (thus 20 per cent).

Transfers on death

On death, tax is recomputed at death rates on all chargeable transfers (and potentially exempt transfers now becoming chargeable) within the last seven years. Thus further IHT, in addition to IHT paid on lifetime transfers during the last seven years, may arise. In addition, a person is deemed to dispose of his estate (including settled property). This is then charged to IHT at the marginal rate (cumulated with the transfers above).

Other planning points

It is imperative that planners ensure that their client's Wills are in order, both from a family and tax point of view.

One way of mitigating IHT exposure is for spouses to bequeath assets up to the value of their respective nil rate bands, presently £150,000, to a discretionary trust. The advantages are:

- The transfer into the trust on the first death should not give rise to any immediate IHT
- The surviving spouse, as one of the beneficiaries, will have access to the capital and income of the trust fund
- The assets in the trust will not form part of the survivor's estate for IHT purposes.

It is also possible for an individual to nominate his/her death in service benefit to a separate discretionary trust and thus ensure that it will remain outside his/her surviving spouse's estate and therefore escape IHT on the second death. However, the capital and income from the fund would be available for the spouse's use during his/her lifetime.

The IHT legislation permits certain gifts to be made free of an immediate charge to tax, other than those noted above. These include an annual exemption for each individual of £3,000, together with an exemption for gifts that comprise normal expenditure out of income and gifts on marriage. An individual could use these exemptions to fund premiums under a life insurance policy, which can be used to meet the eventual IHT liability on death.

Insurance – usually Decreasing Term Assurance, where the amount of cover reduces proportionately to the reduction in the IHT liability – can also be used to protect against IHT liabilities arising on potentially exempt transfers that then lose their potential exemption because death occurs within seven years of the date of the gift.

Finding the story in accounts

What does a journalist use accounts for? Very often, it is to confirm information given by the company in the course of pursuing a story; sometimes, the accounts themselves are the story.

How should you read a set of accounts? Some people start with the cover, which a small but growing number of companies use to hammer home a theme, and then read through the report. Others home in on one particular figure – for instance, operating profit or profit before tax – or focus on one or two key ratios – for example, profit margin (operating profit/sales) or return on net assets (profit before interest/total net assets).

Where one starts really does not matter. What is important is:

- To recognise that financial information is not to be found solely in the profit and loss account and balance sheet, but throughout the whole report
- To look for consistency, that is to say, reinforcement, and, most especially for inconsistency (where, say, the accounts and the chairman's statement do not quite tell the same story) and/or omission (where, say, one or two divisions are mentioned specifically, but not another)
- To have a system, so that your attention is not diverted.

Turning back to the accounts for earlier years, to interim statements and press cuttings, can help detect inconsistency, not apparent from the current year's accounts.

The story behind the figures

Accounting figures need to be put into context. For example, a five per cent fall in sales volume is disappointing, but its significance would be entirely different depending on whether it was the result of:

- A competitor's entry into the market
- A 50 per cent reduction in advertising in order to conserve cash
- A four week strike
- Loss of a major export market due to a strengthening of sterling against the dollar
- A management buy-out of a previously loss-making subsidiary.

What one is trying to do is obtain a dynamic view of the company. How is it (are its fortunes) changing? Why? What is the story behind the figures?

What the figures don't tell you

Accounts suffer from a number of deficiencies. By their very nature, they are a historical record. They tell you what has happened, and not what the future holds.

Annual accounts usually reflect performance over a year – which may consist of periods of very different trading conditions. In a calendar year, business may be growing from January to April, but turn down sharply in May, with an upswing again in the last quarter.

There is growing pressure on companies to produce segmental information (a breakdown of turnover and profit by sector), and a geographical analysis. Where this is provided (as it must for listed companies), it is an important guide to the journalist on the significance of the company's various activities.

Nevertheless, it is often difficult to tell exactly what a company and its various subsidiaries do (for example, whether particular products are manufactured in their entirety, are fabricated from bought-out parts, or purchased in a finished state). It is also often difficult to tell what is made where (for example, where products sold overseas are manufactured) and, thus, how a group is likely to be affected by changes in exchange rates, and in relative cost levels.

Group accounts consolidate (add together) the balance sheets of a company and its subsidiaries; and it is impossible to tell from them where assets are located physically; and whether they are saleable.

This is especially important with regard to cash and bank balances. The accounts do not tell you how easy it would be to remit any cash to the UK, and what tax, if any, would be payable if it were remitted (profits held overseas may be subject to both withholding tax in the overseas country and additional taxation in the UK if they are remitted).

You should also be aware that companies prepare accounts more often than annually. They need to do this, not because of any Stock Exchange or statutory requirement, but from a need for information with which to manage the business. These 'management accounts' are a subset of the broader 'management information', which may include non-financial as well as financial data. It is unlikely that you will be shown, or allowed to see, management accounts since much of their content will be considered confidential. Nonetheless, you should ask what management information can be made available to you.

Beware of brackets () in the profit and loss account. Although the general rule is 'bad news in brackets', some companies use other conventions. This means that it is not always clear on first sight whether the line:

Charge for taxation ***(100)***

means the company has suffered a tax charge of £100 (thousand or million), which is likely, or has received a tax refund of the same amount. Only by working through the numbers can you be sure.

The importance of cash flow

Companies that are unprofitable inevitably fail. But companies that are clearly very profitable sometimes also fail. Why? Because they do not have the cash flow to support their growth.

Published accounts contain a Cash Flow Statement (see chapter on *Financial accounting and reporting*). Although it has some limitations, this is a most useful document. Read it carefully. Talk to management about the company's cash flow; you may find a story here.

What accounts tell you about the future

Strictly, accounts are a record of past stewardship – the directors, the managers of the company, reporting to the shareholders, the owners. In practice, though, the accounts often give clues as to the likely future performance of the company:

- The new style of profit and loss account required by FRS 3 (see chapter on *Financial accounting and reporting*), for example, draws a distinction between turnover and profit generated from discontinued operations and those generated from continuing operations
- Capital commitments, both contracted for and not contracted for, are disclosed in the notes to the accounts
- Creditors due in more than 12 months (and debtors, where they are material) are disclosed, giving some indication of likely future cash flow
- The directors' report, or chairman's statement, may tell you something of the company's plans.

What questions to ask

One does not need to be an accountant to understand accounts. But a knowledge of how accounts are prepared, of company law and accounting standards is essential.

Practice is essential, to enable you better to frame the questions you ask management. Without it, you will be unsure of your ground, and there is a danger that directors and managers will brush you aside as uninformed and your doubts and questions as not deserving of consideration.

Look for patterns, especially patterns that the directors do not mention – for example, the closing over a few months by a supermarket chain of five stores in Northern Scotland. Is this coincidental or a deliberate policy? Are they abandoning the far North? If so, why?

Look for inconsistency. Do they appear to be saying one thing and doing another? Does what they are saying today contradict what they said last year? Why the change?

Ask about the competition. The replies will provide useful background – often a company is prepared to reveal far more of what it knows about its competitors than it will reveal about its own operations, but in doing so it will put its own operations in context.

The company visit

Financial journalists and analysts often have the chance to visit a company and meet its senior management. Such an opportunity should not be turned down lightly; to do so leaves the advantage with the competition. Nor should the company visit be regarded as a perk, as a day out or an escape from the office. Properly conducted, a company visit is hard work.

To take full advantage, prepare thoroughly. The well-informed journalist:

- Has studied the group or company history
- Knows where the main competition lies
- Has considered their plans, strengths and weaknesses
- Has a file of all recent press clippings (at least a year) regarding the company and its main competitors.

More than that, he has already framed a number of pertinent questions to which he would like the answer – which he may or may not raise publicly.

The art is to listen, rather than to talk. To keep the flow going, rather than bring it to a premature halt. In a small group, it pays to grunt, or say "Yes", or raise one's eyebrows in mild disbelief, rather than interrupt the speaker. Few people, being interviewed, can resist a questioning look, or an unfilled silence. They tend to go on, to explain, to amplify, to defend themselves and their company. Listen for nuances. Store them up for possible use later, rather than pounce immediately.

Do not allow a speaker who says "There are three reasons why we did so and so" to be interrupted and give only two. The third reason might just be the most revealing.

Take advantage of any offer or opportunity to view the factory and offices – indeed, actively seek such an opportunity. This again is not simply an interesting trip or a diversion, it is an opportunity:

- To use your eyes: How old is the plant and machinery? Is it general purpose or special purpose machinery? Is the company committed to one product or is there flexibility? Is it well maintained? Will it produce to high accuracy? How well is the plant loaded? Is there an urgent need to sell more? Does the plant look efficient? Or is there evidence, or even a feeling, of waste and inefficiency?
- To use your ears: Telephones that ring and are not answered tell one something of the organisation one is visiting – that customers, and potential customers, do not matter, that top management does not see the importance of efficient, considerate customer relations, does not care, or has more important things to worry about (for example, labour relations). Staff are not always discreet. They may mention, in your hearing, intentionally or more probably unintentionally, new products for which there are great hopes, or old products on the way out. Do you follow up such indiscretions by direct questions? Not if the only chance of being given the information is 'off the record'. And certainly not when you are part of a large group, simply to show how clever you are. Instead, take the opportunity, after the visit, to write a thank you note to your host; and ask your question in that, so, hopefully obtaining a personal reply, and at the same time building a contact
- To interpret 'body language': How do managers behave to one another, and in one another's presence? Do they suggest, at one extreme, an autocratic chairman or chief executive who will brook no dissent, or at the other, a middle management that has the confidence of the board, and feels free to speak up and where necessary to act on its own initiative? On the factory floor, does the chief executive do all the talking, with the foreman and machine operators standing dutifully to attention? Or are you allowed to talk directly to the machine operator?

It is sometimes said of an accountant that he has 'auditor's eyes' – that he is able to spot the inconsistencies, that somehow he knows where to look. This is not something one can acquire from a text book, nor is it simply born of experience. It is a combination of dissatisfaction, suspicion, restlessness and of many skills, not least an ability continually to put two and two together in the knowledge, and expectation, that very occasionally they will make five.

As a final thought on the company visit, it is a useful discipline to make notes at the time and immediately on return to write them up into a file note.

Sources of information

If you are to become a specialist, it is essential to have not only a good library, but one's own personal sources. Build these as fast and as widely as you can.

Sources of information provided by the company of interest to the journalist are:

- Half-yearly (and in a few cases, quarterly) reports;
- Prospectuses, listing particulars, and circulars on acquisitions and disposals: These often provide information that is not available from any other source
- Form 20-F and other filings (if the company is listed in the US)
- Company newsletters and magazines: The impression given to employees may be subtly different from that given to shareholders
- Catalogues and sales information
- Annual meetings: City editors, from time to time, acquire a small holding in a company so as to be able to ask questions at the annual meeting.

External sources include:

- Datastream
- Extel Cards
- Hambro Company Guide
- ICC Datacards
- Keynotes (published by ICC)
- McCarthy Information Services
- Reuters Textline
- Government statistical publications.

Doing your own research at Companies House

Companies are required to file the following information with the Registrar of Companies:

- Copies of their Memorandum and Articles of Association
- Details of registered office, directors, share capital and debentures and mortgages
- An Annual Return that contains *inter alia* either a full list of members (every third year) or a list of changes since the last return
- A list of all subsidiaries.

Listed companies are required by the Stock Exchange to file a copy of their annual report and accounts within six months, though this can be extended somewhat in the case of a company with overseas interests.

Companies' files are maintained at Cardiff, but they can be inspected on microfiche either at Cardiff, or at 55 City Road, London EC1 1BB, on payment of a fee of £3.00 per company. The microfiche can be viewed at Companies House but belongs to, and may be taken away by, the searcher. Although Companies House (in both locations) is open from 9.00 am to 5.00 pm, the latest time for making application for a company search is 3.00 pm, since developing the microfiche film takes about an hour and a half.

A search may also be made by post to the Cardiff Office (Crown Way, Maindy, Cardiff CF4 3UZ) for £4.00 per company. Hard copy costs £5.50 per document.

There are a number of search agents who will provide the service on payment of a fee – look in the Yellow Pages for names.

How to use brokers' reports

Brokers' analysts and fund managers have opportunities, and sources, not available to the financial journalist. They make far more company visits, and can often field a team rather than a single individual. They also have more opportunity to specialise than a journalist, whose field of expertise frequently has to be far wider.

Brokers' assessments of a company or sector thus provide a useful source of information. Strictly, they should not reveal anything that is not publicly available, but they invariably do. They are an especially valuable source of information on:

- Individual business segments
- Future plans
- The possible outturn for a period.

Beware, however, of two problem areas:

- Brokers can differ widely on likely profits, especially where, as with the banks, considerable provision for doubtful debts are required
- Where a firm acts as a broker to a company on which it is reporting, take any assertions of strength with a pinch of salt, especially where they do not reflect market opinion.

Glossary

Accounting bases: The bases of valuation adopted in the preparation of financial statements – for example, the historical cost basis, under which all assets, liabilities, costs and income are stated at the money amount involved at the date of the transaction.

Accounting concepts: There are four fundamental accounting concepts. Financial statements are presumed to have been prepared on the basis of these, unless otherwise specified. The concepts are:

- Accruals concept
- Consistency concept
- Going concern concept
- Prudence concept.

Accounting policies: The specific methods of accounting for particular transactions chosen by a company from those prescribed or permitted by law or accounting standards for use in the preparation of financial statements.

Accruals concept: One of the four fundamental accounting concepts under which income is matched with the costs incurred in earning it, regardless of the actual timing of cash flows.

Acquisition accounting: A method of accounting, distinguished from merger accounting, used to account for business combinations. Acquisition accounting works on the basis of the acquisition of one entity by another, resulting in goodwill being the difference between the consideration paid for the acquisition and the fair value of the net assets acquired.

Administration: A legal state during which a company receives the protection of the courts while it reorganises its affairs, free from pressure from creditors.

Advance Corporation Tax (ACT): Corporation tax paid by a UK company, in advance of its mainstream corporation tax liability, on the payment of dividends to its shareholders.

Annual General Meeting (AGM): A meeting of the shareholders of a company prescribed by law to be held at least once in every calendar year. A private company may dispense with it.

Annuity: An annual payment, often from an investment that pays a fixed or determinate amount (which may comprise part income and part repayment of capital).

Arbitrage: Buying and selling currency, Bills of Exchange etc in different markets so as to take advantage of different rates in each market.

Articles of Association: One of two documents that comprise a company's 'constitution'; the other is the Memorandum of Association. The Articles set out the detailed management of the company and the rights of shareholders.

Asset: In accounting terms, items that confer economic benefit to the owner and therefore can be given a monetary value.

Audit: An examination of financial statements that includes verification of the accounting records and tests of controls, so that an independent opinion may be given as to the truth and fairness of the company's financial statements and other matters required by law.

Authorised capital: The maximum amount of share capital that a company may issue.

Bed and breakfasting: Sale and repurchase transaction within/during a Stock Exchange account period, with a view to realising inherent gains or losses, usually for Capital Gains Tax purposes.

Bonus issue: An issue of shares free of charge to shareholders, paid from retained earnings.

Capital allowances: Tax deductions in respect of capital expenditure on plant and machinery (or industrial buildings), substituted in a tax computation for depreciation (and usually calculated on a different basis).

Central Bank: Usually an organ of government, charged with the maintenance of the currency and management of the domestic economy.

Certificates of deposit (CD): Bearer documents representing deposits with banks. Because they are bearer documents (payable to the holder), they are negotiable instruments.

Chargeable gains: The amount of the profit or gain on sale of a capital asset by a company that is chargeable to corporation tax.

Clearing bank: A bank that operates, or is party to the operation of, a system whereby cheques drawn on different banks are settled on an overall rather than individual basis.

Close company: A tax definition of a company deemed to be under the control of a limited number of shareholders, or its directors.

Collective investment schemes: Schemes that pool a large number of small investments, providing the small investor with the same ability to diversify his investment portfolio and access to the same quality of investment advice as large investors.

Consistency concept: One of the four fundamental accountancy concepts, under which like items are treated in a like manner, both in the same set of financial statements and over time.

Contracts for differences: Buying and selling stocks and shares within/during the same Stock Exchange account period with no intention of taking or effecting delivery of the shares but merely paying or receiving the differences between the two prices. Such contracts are treated as a wager and so are governed by wagering contracts.

Currency risk: The risk of loss arising in respect of a holding of foreign currency (or of foreign assets) in the event of a fluctuation in exchange rates.

Current assets: Trading assets, held for resale.

Current cost accounts: Financial statements prepared under SSAP 16 (now withdrawn), with the intention of providing for the effect of inflation.

Debentures: A long term loan to a company, evidenced by a trust deed and certificates.

Deferred taxation: Additional taxation charged (or credited) in company accounts to smooth the impact of timing differences arising from the different treatment of items in financial statements and tax computations (this applies particularly in respect of capital allowances).

Discount: The amount by which a buying or selling price is lower than the nominal price.

Domestic markets: Internal markets between local banks within a single currency.

Double tax treaty: An agreement between two countries designed to ensure that a taxpayer of one who receives income from the second is not subject to taxation twice.

Earnings per share (EPS): A figure, published in financial statements whose method of calculation is specified in SSAP 3 (as amended by FRS 3), based on the division of the profits earned by a company by the number of shares entitled to receive dividends out of those profits.

Equity: Capital introduced by shareholders or retained in the company on their behalf.

Eurobond: A bond issued and sold to investors outside the country in whose currency the bond is denominated. Usually, Eurobonds are issued for amounts in excess of $100m and have a life of at least 3 years.

Eurocommercial paper (ECP): A short term credit note (debt instrument) issued under the umbrella of a medium term facility.

Eurodollar: US dollars held in a $ account in a European bank.

Exchange: The process of converting one currency or asset into another. An exchange is also used to describe the place (or market) where such a conversion occurs.

Exchange rate: The value of one currency in terms of another.

Extraordinary General Meeting (EGM): A meeting of the shareholders of a company, called by the shareholders or the directors, to discuss a topic specified in the notice of the meeting.

Factoring: A form of working capital finance, based on advancing sums of money on the security of future receipts from debtors.

Finance lease: An accounting term, distinguished from 'operating lease', where the lessee takes substantially all the risks and rewards of ownership and thus the transaction is treated as if the lessee had acquired the asset in a purchase transaction.

Financial future: A forward position in foreign currency or monetary assets taken by the holder to protect himself (hedge) against a future currency, exchange or interest rate risk.

Financial Reporting Exposure Drafts (FREDs): Documents issued by the Accounting Standards Board for consultation in advance of the publication of a Financial Reporting Standard.

Financial Reporting Standards (FRSs): Documents issued by the Accounting Standards Board that set out the manner of accounting for the transaction(s) that form the topic of the standard, and are mandatory on preparers and auditors of company financial statements.

Fixed assets: Assets held for their use in the business, rather than for resale.

Floating rate note (FRN): A Eurobond whose interest rate can be altered periodically according to terms agreed when the bond was purchased.

Flotation: The process of gaining a Stock Exchange quotation for a company for the first time, usually involving the issue of shares.

Foreign bank: A bank headquartered outside the UK.

Forward: When one buys or sells a currency for delivery on a future date, one is said to have sold (bought) forward.

Forward market: Buying or selling foreign currency for receipt at a future date.

Forward rate agreement (FRA): An agreement between two parties fixing the interest rate for a period commencing at a future date, usually within the next 12 months.

Futures: Commodities, stocks, monetary assets or currency bought or sold for future delivery.

Gearing: The ratio between equity and debt in the capital structure of a company. In the US, gearing is known as 'leverage'.

Gilt edged securities: Government securities that yield interest, generally regarded as low risk investments.

Going concern concept: One of the four fundamental accounting concepts, under which a company is presumed to be able to continue in existence for at least twelve months from the balance sheet date.

Goodwill: An intangible asset, represented by the excess of the purchase price over the fair value of the net assets, arising on the acquisition of a business by another.

Government bonds: Bonds issued by the government, which can be bought and sold on the stock market.

Government securities: Loans raised by the government, which can be bought and sold on the stock market.

Group relief: A system of tax relief that enables a group of companies to set off revenue losses in one UK group company against profits in another, thereby reducing the overall group tax charge.

Hedge: To protect against movements in prices or exchange rates through complementary transactions.

Historical cost convention: An accounting base, under which assets are accounted for at their cost on acquisition, regardless of later increases in value.

Independent taxation: A system of income tax that provides for the separate taxation of income of husband and wife, with personal allowances and reliefs transferable between the couple.

Indexation: A process of applying an index (often the Retail Prices Index) to original cost, so as to reduce the chargeable gain for capital gains tax or corporation tax purposes.

Insider dealing: Illegal dealing in shares by a person with knowledge obtained from his position with the company.

Intangible assets: Assets that have no tangible form, such as brands and goodwill.

Interbank market: Used for raising short and medium term funding and placing excess funds. Terms range from one day to five years, with shorter maturities more common. Usually takes the form of a market between local banks within a country (see Domestic markets) but Eurocurrency markets, which are international, are also interbank markets.

Interest rate risk: The risk of loss arising in respect of a monetary asset in the event of a movement in interest rates.

Interim accounts: Abbreviated and unaudited financial statements issued by quoted companies in compliance with Stock Exchange regulations, following the completion of the first six months trading each year.

Invoice discounting: Similar to factoring, except that it can operate on the basis of individual (usually, high value) invoices rather than the full sales ledger.

Issued capital: The actual amount of share capital issued by a company.

Junk bonds: High yielding bonds used to finance highly leveraged acquisitions, the high yield reflecting the level of risk. The junk bond market was established by Drexel Burnham Lambert in New York in the early 1980s.

Leasing: A means of financing fixed asset purchases 'off balance sheet'. A bank (or other lessor) purchases the asset and leases it to the user for a monthly payment, part interest and part capital. For accounting purposes, leases are divided into 'finance leases', where the lessee has substantially all the risks and rewards of ownership, and 'operating leases', which are more akin to hiring.

Leverage: See 'Gearing'.

Liability: The value of claims against a company/group due for settlement within a specific time.

Limited liability: A legal state in which the owner of a business is not held liable for the properly incurred debts of the business in the event of its failure. Usually found as 'limited liability company' (Ltd.) or 'public limited company' (plc), where the members' liability is limited to amounts unpaid on shares held by them.

Liquidation: The dissolution, or winding up, of a limited company.

Liquidity: Availability of cash.

Listing: A quotation on The Stock Exchange.

Management accounts: Accounts prepared by the management of a business for their own use in running the business.

Management Buy-In (MBI): Where a team of managers, who have not previously worked in the business, buy the shares of the owners with the help of bank financing and thus 'take over' the business.

Management Buy-Out (MBO): Where a team of managers who work in a business buys the shares of the owners and thus takes over the business.

Management information: Financial and non-financial information prepared by management for their own use in running the business.

Margin: The difference between the purchase price and the selling price of an asset. Also used to refer to a profit.

Memorandum of Association: With the Articles of Association, one of the two documents making up a company's 'constitution'. The Memorandum sets the broad scope of the company's activities.

Merchant bank: Historically the financiers of trade; nowadays involved in corporate finance.

Merger accounting: A method of accounting for business combinations, which is based on the fact that no resources leave the combined group and thus allows the two businesses to be accounted for together as if they had always been together.

Mezzanine finance: Forms of finance that share the characteristics of debt and equity. Preference share capital is an example.

Minority interests: Where a subsidiary is not 100 per cent owned by the parent, the other shareholders are the 'minority interest'.

Money market: The market for liquid financial instruments; the wholesale market in which banks borrow, lend or invest money.

Net asset value (NAV): The total value of a company's assets, less its liabilities, often expressed on a 'per share' basis.

Non-executive director: A director who does not work in the business and thus is 'independent'.

Objects: The purpose(s) for which a company is established. They usually form the third clause in a company's Memorandum of Association.

Off balance sheet finance: Forms of finance that are constructed so that, if a strict legal interpretation is applied, they will not appear as borrowings on a company's balance sheet. Accounting standards have proscribed most methods of off balance sheet finance.

On margin: The practice of putting up only a portion of the full price of a contract, thereby trading largely on credit. A characteristic of trading on LIFFE.

Open outcry: A system employed in certain markets (for instance, the LIFFE) to match purchasers with sellers on a person-to-person basis.

Operating and financial review: A statement of a company's performance and plans for the future proposed to be included in the annual financial statements by a non-mandatory statement issued by the Accounting Standards Board in 1993.

Operating lease: In accounting terms, a form of lease akin to hiring, as distinguished from a 'finance lease'.

Options: The right to buy or sell an asset at a predetermined price at a given point in time.

Ordinary shares: The normal equity investment in a limited company.

Par: The face value, generally of stocks and shares.

Placing: An issue of shares that the sponsoring stockbroker arranges to be taken up by his clients.

Polarisation: A concept introduced by the Financial Services Act, 1986 whereby a person may act either as an independent adviser or as a tied agent selling the products of a single company, but not both.

Preference shares: A form of share capital that receives preference in the payment of dividends and/or repayment of capital on the winding up of a business. For this security, a lower return is often received, frequently at a predetermined fixed rate.

Preliminary figures: Abbreviated, though audited, figures released by a quoted company before its financial statements are published.

Premium: An amount paid by the lessee to the lessor for the grant of a lease over property. With regard to the issue of shares, it is the amount over the par value paid by a subscriber for the shares. In an insurance context, it is the amount paid by the insured party to secure insurance cover.

Price earnings ratio (P/E): A expression of the number of times current earnings are contained in the price paid or quoted for a share.

Principal: The amount of a loan on which interest is (generally) payable.

Prior year adjustment: An adjustment to the financial statements of a previous year, permitted only in specified circumstances, and shown by way of adjusting the opening balance forward on retained profits.

Private company: As distinguished from a public company, a private company may have as few as one shareholder and may not sell or offer its shares to the general public. If it has limited liability, it would normally be designated 'Ltd.'.

Promissory note: A signed document promising to pay a certain amount, either on demand or at some future date. A bank note is an example of a promissory note.

Prospectus: A legal document issued when raising finance for a public company through a share issue, the contents of which are subject to strict regulation.

Prudence concept: One of the four fundamental accounting concepts, under which profits are not recognised until earned and losses are provided for when foreseen.

Public limited company: Contrasted with a private company, a public company must have a minimum of seven shareholders, an issued share capital of £50,000 of which a quarter must be paid up, and may raise capital from the general public by means of a prospectus. Usually designated as 'plc', or some variation thereof.

Review: Often performed by the auditors on a company's interim accounts, a review consists of analytical procedures and discussions with management. A review involves substantially less in scope than an audit.

Rights issue: An issue of shares offered to existing shareholders who, if they all take up their allocation, will retain their existing relative shareholding.

Roll over: In the context of a loan or other similar form of finance, roll over can occur when one loan is effectively cancelled and replaced by another.

Rollover relief: A form of relief from capital gains tax under which gains on the disposal of one asset reinvested in business property are not taxed immediately, but deferred until eventually realised on the disposal of the second asset.

Self Regulatory Organisation (SRO): A body recognised by the Securities and Investment Board under the Financial Services Act, 1986 for the regulation of specific groups of market players.

Settlement: The completion of a transaction, when delivery of the securities to the buyer and payment to the seller has been achieved.

Shareholders' funds: The total of share capital and retained profits shown on a company's balance sheet.

Spot market: Trading that requires immediate delivery and payment, though usually 'immediately' is defined as being within two days.

Statements of Recommended Practice (SORPs): Non-mandatory methods of accounting issued by relevant industry groupings with the approval of the (then) Accounting Standards Committee.

Statements of Standard Accounting Practice (SSAPs): Mandatory statements of accounting methods issued by the (then) Accounting Standards Committee and promulgated by the six major accounting bodies.

Subsidiary undertaking: A company, partnership or unincorporated association in which the parent controls the majority of the voting rights or the majority of the directors' votes.

Swaps: An agreement between two parties to exchange one set of cash flows for another.

Syndicated loan: A loan provided by more than one bank, acting under a 'lead' banker.

Tangible fixed assets: Fixed assets with physical characteristics, such as property.

Treasury: The function of managing a business' liquidity, making sure funds are available to meet liabilities and surplus funds are earning a return. Treasury also monitors and maintains within acceptable limits the business' exposure to movements in exchange and interest rates.

Ultra vires: Actions outside a company's 'objects', which render the directors personally liable for any resulting debts.

Underwriting: The process of subscribing for share capital or of sharing an insurance risk.

Venture capital: Funds provided by financiers on a 'high risk, high return' basis.

Warrants: Instruments attached to bonds, though tradable separately, entitling the holder to buy either equity in the company or further bonds.

Acronyms

AAPA	Association of Authorised Practising Accountants
ACCA	Chartered Association of Certified Accountants
ACT	Advance Corporation Tax
AFBD	Association of Futures Brokers and Dealers
AGM	Annual General Meeting
APACS	Association of Payment Clearing Services
APT	Automated Pit Trading
ASB	Accounting Standards Board
ASC	Accounting Standards Committee
ATOM	Automated Trading and Order Matching
AVC	Additional Voluntary Contribution
BACS	Bankers Automated Clearing Services
BBA	British Bankers' Association
BBAIRS	British Bankers' Association Interest Rate Swap
BES	Business Expansion Scheme
BVCA	British Venture Capital Association
CBI	Confederation of British Industry
CBT	Chicago Board of Trade
CCAB	Consultative Committee of Accounting Bodies
CDs	Certificates of Deposit
CFC	Controlled foreign company
CGT	Capital Gains Tax
CHAPS	Clearing House Automated Payment System
CLCB	Committee of London Clearing Bankers
CLSB	Committee of London and Scottish Bankers
CME	Chicago Mercantile Exchange
CNS	Company News Service
DTI	Department of Trade and Industry
ECP	Eurocommercial Paper
EGM	Extraordinary General Meeting
EZ	Enterprise Zones
FIB	Family Income Bond
FIMBRA	Financial Intermediaries, Managers and Brokers' Regulatory Association
FOX	Futures and Options Exchange
FRABBA	Forward Rate Agreement British Bankers' Association
FRA	Forward Rate Agreements
FRC	Financial Reporting Council

FRED	Financial Reporting Exposure Draft
FRN	Floating Rate Note
FRRP	Financial Reporting Review Panel
FRS	Financial Reporting Standard
FSA	Financial Services Act
FT	Financial Times
FT-30	Financial Times Ordinary Share (index)
FT-A	Financial Times - Actuaries All-Share (index)
FT-SE	Financial Times - Stock Exchange
FT-SE 100	Financial Times - Stock Exchange 100 (index)
HP	Hire purchase
ICAEW	Institute of Chartered Accountants in England & Wales
ICAI	Institute of Chartered Accountants in Ireland
ICAS	Institute of Chartered Accountants of Scotland
ICCH	International Commodity Clearing House
IHT	Inheritance Tax
IMM	International Monetary Market (of Chicago Mercantile Exchange)
IMRO	Investment Managers Regulatory Organisation
ISDA	International Swap Dealers Association
ISE	International Stock Exchange
LAUTRO	Life Assurance and Unit Trust Regulatory Organisation
LCE	London Commodity Exchange
LFOX	London Futures and Options Exchange
LIBID	London Interbank Bid Rate
LIBOR	London Interbank Offered Rate
LIFFE	London International Financial Futures Exchange
LIMEAN	London Interbank Mean Rate
LME	London Metal Exchange
LPSO	Lloyds Policy Signing Office
M&A	Mergers and acquisitions
MBI	Management Buy-In
MBO	Management Buy-Out
MMC	Monopolies and Mergers Commission
NASDIM	National Association of Security Dealers and Investment Managers
NMS	Normal Market Size
NPV	Net present value
NYFE	New York Futures Exchange
OFT	Office of Fair Trading
ORIE	Overseas Recognised Investment Exchange
OTC	Over-the-Counter
PAYE	Pay As You Earn
P/E	Price/earnings ratio
PEP	Personal Equity Plan

PET	Potentially Exempt Transfer
PHI	Permanent Health Insurance
PIA	Personal Investment Authority
PIV	Periodic Inspection Visit
PLC	Public Limited Company
PPP	Personal Pension Plan
PTC	Periodicals Training Council
RAP	Retirement Annuity Policy
RIE	Recognised Investment Exchange
RNS	Regulatory News Service
RPB	Recognised Professional Body
RPI	Retail Prices Index
SEAF	SEAQ Automated Execution Facility
SEAQ	Stock Exchange Automated Quotation
SEPON	Stock Exchange Pool Nominees
SFA	Securities and Futures Association
SFO	Serious Fraud Office
SIB	Securities and Investments Board
SORP	Statement of Recommended Practice
SRO	Self-Regulatory Organisation
SSAP	Statement of Standard Accounting Practice
TALISMAN	Transfer Accounting, Lodgement for Investors, Stock Management for Principals
TESSA	Tax Exempt Special Savings Accounts
TSA	The Securities Association
UITF	Urgent Issues Task Force
USD	US Dollars
USM	Unlisted Securities Market
VAT	Value Added Tax

Directory

Accounting Standards Board
Holborn Hall, 100 Grays Inn Road, London WC1X 8AL
071 404 8818

Association of British Factors
24-28 Bloomsbury Way, London WC1A 2PX
071 831 4268

Association of British Insurers
Aldermary House, Queen Street, London EC4N 1TT
071 248 4477

Association of Investment Trust Companies
Park House, 16 Finsbury Circus, London EC2M 7JJ
071 588 5347

Auditing Practices Board
Moorgate Place, London EC2P 2BJ
071 628 7060

Baltic Exchange
24 St Mary Axe, London EC3A 8EP
071 623 5501

Baltic Futures Exchange
24 St Mary Axe, London EC3A 8EP
071 283 5146

Bank of England
Threadneedle Street, London EC2R 8AH
071 601 4444

British Bankers' Association
10 Lombard Street, London EC3V 9AR
071 623 4001

British Insurance and Investment Brokers' Association
BIIBA House, 14 Bevis Marks, London EC3A 7NT
071 623 9043

British Invisible Exports Council
Windsor House, 39 King Street, London EC2V 8DQ
071 600 1198

British Merchant Banking and Securities Houses Association
6 Frederick's Place, Old Jewry, London EC2R 8BT
071 796 3606

British Venture Capital Association
1 Surrey Street, London WC2R 2PS
071 836 5702

Building Societies Association
3 Saville Row, London W1X 1AF
071 437 0655

Chartered Association of Certified Accountants
29 Lincoln's Inn Fields, London WC2A 3EE
071 242 6855

Chartered Institute of Management Accountants
63 Portland Place, London W1N 4AB
071 637 2311

Chartered Institute of Public Finance and Accountancy
3 Robert Street, London WC2N 6BH
071 895 8823

Data Protection Registrar
Wycliffe House, Water Lane, Wilmslow, Cheshire, SK9 5AF
0625 535777

Department of Trade and Industry
1 Victoria Street, London SW1H 0ET
071 215 7877

Equipment Leasing Association
18 Upper Grosvenor Street, London W1X 9PB
071 491 2783

Federation of Commodity Associations
1 Commodity Quay, St Katharine's Dock, London E1 9AX
071 481 2080

Finance Houses Association
18 Upper Grosvenor Street, London W1X 9PB
071 491 2783

Financial Intermediaries, Managers and Brokers Regulatory Association
Hertsmere House, Hertsmere Road, London E14 4AB
071 538 8860

Institute of Chartered Accountants in England & Wales
Chartered Accountants Hall, Moorgate Place, London EC2P 2BJ
071 920 8100

Institute of Chartered Accountants in Ireland
87/89 Pembroke Road, Ballsbridge, Dublin 4
010 353 1 680400

Institute of Chartered Accountants of Scotland
27 Queen Street, Edinburgh, EH2 1LA
031 225 5673

International Accounting Standards Committee
167 Fleet Street, London EC4A 2ES
071 353 0565

International Petroleum Exchange
Cereal House, 58 Mark Lane, London EC3R 7NE
071 481 2080

Investment Management Regulatory Organisation
Broadwalk House, 5 Appold Street, London EC2A 2LL
071 628 6022

Law Society
113 Chancery Lane, London WC2A 1PL
071 242 1222

Life Assurance and Unit Trust Regulatory Organisation
Centre Point, 103 New Oxford Street, London W1
071 379 0444

Lloyds'
1 Lime Street, London EC3M 7HA
071 623 7100

London Commodities Exchange
1 Commodity Quay, St Katharine's Docks, London E1 9AX
071 481 2080

London Discount Market Association
39 Cornhill, London EC3V 3NU
071 623 1020

London Futures and Options Exchange
1 Commodity Quay, St Katharine's Docks, London E1 9AX
071 481 2080

London International Financial Futures Exchange
Royal Exchange, Cornhill, London EC3V 3PJ
071 623 0444

London Metal Exchange
Plantation House, Fenchurch Street, London EC3M 3AP
071 626 3311

Monopolies & Mergers Commission
New Court, 48 Carey Street, London WC2A 2JP
071 324 1468

National Association of Pension Funds
12-18 Grosvenor Gardens, London SW1W 0DH
071 730 0585

Office of Fair Trading
Field House, 15-25 Bream's Buildings, London EC4A 1PR
071 242 2858

Panel on Takeovers and Mergers
Stock Exchange Building, Old Broad Street, London EC2P 2JX
071 382 9026

Registrar of Companies
Companies House, 55 City Road, London EC1Y 1BB
071 253 9393
Companies House, Crown Way, Maindy, Cardiff CF4 3UZ
0222 388588

Registry of Friendly Societies
15 Great Marlborough Street, London W1V 2AX
071 437 9992

Securities and Futures Authority
Cottons Centre, Cottons Lane, London SE1 2QB
071 378 9000

Securities and Investments Board
Gavrelle House, 2-14 Bunhill Row, London EC1Y 8RA
071 638 1240

Serious Fraud Office
Elm House, Elm Street, London WC1X 0BJ
071 239 7272

Stock Exchange
Old Broad Street, London EC2N 1HP
071 588 2355

Unit Trust Association
London House, 53-54 Haymarket, London SW1Y 4RP
071 930 4241

Index

Compiled by Julitta Clancy

E

G

W

Y